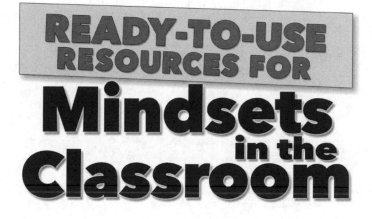

READY-TO-USE RESOURCES FOR
Mindsets in the Classroom

B

READY-TO-USE RESOURCES FOR

Mindsets in the Classroom

Everything Educators Need for Building Growth Mindset Learning Communities

Mary Cay Ricci

PRUFROCK PRESS INC.
WACO, TEXAS

Library of Congress Cataloging-in-Publication Data

Ricci, Mary Cay, 1960-
 Ready-to-use resources for mindsets in the classroom : everything educators need for building growth mindset learning communities / by Mary Cay Ricci.
   pages cm
 Companion to: Mindsets in the classroom.
 ISBN 978-1-61821-396-9 (pbk.)
 1. Learning, Psychology of. 2. Academic achievement. 3. Motivation in education. I. Ricci, Mary Cay, 1960- Mindsets in the classroom. II. Title.
 LB1060.R496 2015
 370.15'23--dc23
                    2015010391

Edited by Lacy Compton

Cover and layout design by Raquel Trevino

ISBN-13: 978-1-61821-396-9

At the time of this book's publication, all facts and figures cited are the most current available. All telephone numbers, addresses, and website URLs are accurate and active. All publications, organizations, websites, and other resources exist as described in the book, and all have been verified. The author and Prufrock Press Inc. make no warranty or guarantee concerning the information and materials given out by organizations or content found at websites, and we are not responsible for any changes that occur after this book's publication. If you find an error, please contact Prufrock Press Inc.

Prufrock Press Inc.
P.O. Box 8813
Waco, TX 76714-8813
Phone: (800) 998-2208
Fax: (800) 240-0333
http://www.prufrock.com

TABLE OF CONTENTS

Acknowledgements

I would like to thank the following people for support and contribution to this book.

Thanks for welcoming me into your schools:

- ⊛ Kristen Canning, Principal, Kemptown Elementary, Frederick County, MD
- ⊛ Karen Gregory, Principal, Maryvale Elementary School, Montgomery County, MD
- ⊛ Christine Roberts and Susan Harris, Dumbarton Middle School, Baltimore County, MD

Thanks for sharing your terrific book study models:

- ⊛ Eric Ewald, Principal, Riverside Elementary, Iowa
- ⊛ Antoine Spencer, Principal, Otto Middle School, Plano, TX
- ⊛ Emmanuel André, STAT Teacher, Owings Mills High School, Baltimore County, MD
- ⊛ Christine Roberts STAT Teacher, Dumbarton Middle School, Baltimore County, MD

Thanks to Wisconsin CESA 7 Mindset in the Classroom Attendees for sharing some new extended text ideas.

Thanks for sharing your ideas and your growth mindset student stories:

- ⊛ Frederick County Primary Talent Development Teachers:
- ⊛ Elizabeth Brohawn
- ⊛ Lisa Long
- ⊛ Barbara Rudakevych
- ⊛ Michelle Keegin
- ⊛ Kristin Ratkowski
- ⊛ Angela Thomas
- ⊛ Brenda Kurtianyk
- ⊛ Erin Miller
- ⊛ Carol Bates, FCPS Teacher Specialist

Special thanks to Meg Lee, Supervisor of Advanced Academics, Frederick County Public Schools, MD, for being an extra set of eyes and always asking the right questions to spark my thinking further. I appreciate all you do.

CHAPTER 1

WHAT ARE MINDSETS, AND HOW DO THEY AFFECT THE CLASSROOM?

What are mindsets? Thanks to the research of Dr. Carol Dweck, Stanford University professor of psychology, education is going through a shift in thinking about student learning and intelligence. Dweck (2006) described a belief system that asserts that intelligence can be developed and coined the term *growth mindset*. Educators with a growth mindset believe that all students can achieve at higher levels—with effort, perseverance, and resiliency. Learners with a growth mindset believe that they can grow their intelligence with hard work. A growth mindset learning environment encapsulates the philosophy that there is enough success for everyone and both teachers and students learn about the malleability of the brain and what can happen as a result of practice, perseverance, resiliency, and grit.

Conversely, Dweck used the term *fixed mindset*, which is a belief system in which one believes that intelligence is something you are born with—it is innate and although everyone can learn new things, your innate intelligence cannot be changed. A person with a fixed mindset might believe that he or she has predetermined "smarts" or talents in a particular area, but not in other areas. A student with a fixed mindset might believe that he or she will never be good in a particular subject or be afraid to try something that he or she thinks is too difficult or at which he or she fears failure.

The growth mindset that has been demonstrated by educators across a myriad of education levels and content areas over the past few years is both impressive and rejuvenating. I have been fortunate to work with schools, school districts, and district leadership teams across the country since the release of *Mindsets in the Classroom: Building a Culture of Success and Student Achievement in Schools* (Ricci, 2013) and have been amazed by the commitment that educators have toward building a growth mindset culture in schools and districts. Even though the purpose of my visits is to guide and educate, it is I who have learned. These experiences have allowed even more clarity as to what we must do as educators to continue to develop growth mindset schools and school districts so that all adults and students are provided with opportunities and so they believe that they can succeed with perseverance, effort, and motivation.

This book will provide resources that will help educators move forward in their growth mindset journey and serves as a partner book to *Mindsets in the Classroom*. The chapter resources mirror the chapter content of the original book.

Since the release of *Mindsets of the Classroom*, many educators have approached me and asked to identify the most important components of a growth mindset learning environment. In other words, what are the most important actions that must occur in order to have a growth mindset classroom? After much listening, observing, research, and reflection, I have identified four components that are essential to a growth mindset culture. These are areas that each learning environment should strive to obtain. These cannot happen overnight and sometimes not even within one school year. These actions should be a long-term commitment and educators must have a growth mindset themselves in order to persevere to attain these goals. These four components are:

1. equitable access to advanced learning opportunities;
2. deliberate cultivation of psychosocial skills such as perseverance, resiliency, and grit;
3. student understanding of neural networks in the brain; and
4. growth mindset feedback and praise.

Throughout this resource book, you will find tools that will help implement these actions, but for now, let's break these down a little.

Equitable Access to Advanced Learning Opportunities

Do all of the students in your class, school, or district have access to enriched and accelerated learning? Is a label (such as "GT") a requirement to access these opportunities? Ongoing informal assessment and observation should allow for all students, not just those with already developed abilities, to participate in advanced learning opportunities. This may be teacher facilitated small-group work within the classroom or an advanced class offering at the secondary level. Teachers must have a growth mindset in order to allow this to happen. No gatekeeping, no barriers, no "sorry but you are not 'ready' for this."

Once students have this access, are supports put in place to help students succeed? On a recent visit with a group of high school teachers, they proudly announced that they have open access to all of their Honors and AP classes. Any student who wants to enroll may enroll. My momentary happiness did not last long—they shared that most of those students who self-enroll without the recommendation of a teacher don't "make it" in the class. After some discussion, two things were determined; first, the Honors and AP classes were not at all responsive or differentiated to meet students' needs. The teachers just instructed the whole class as if all of the 25+ kids were on the same level. Second, they possessed a complete "sink or swim" mentality. The attitude was that if the student was in the class, he or she should be able to handle it. No supports or scaffolds were in place for a student who struggled. In fact, in many cases, the child was counseled to move to a standard level class at the first sign of struggle. (On a side note, struggle is not necessarily a bad thing. It is actually a good experience for a student to struggle because resiliency cannot be developed without experiencing some degree of struggle . . . more about that later.) With equitable access, provisions should be in place to help students succeed.

Deliberate Cultivation of Psychosocial Skills

Many educators do not realize that approximately 75% of achievement is contributed to psychosocial skills (which some researchers refer to as noncognitive factors) and only approximately 25% of innate intelligence or IQ contributes to achievement (Olszewski-Kubilius, 2013). The cultivation of these skills is imperative, especially for those students who have not yet developed their abilities and/or talents. The skills that must be deliberately modeled, taught, and cultivated include but are not limited to: perseverance, resiliency, grit, emotional regulation, comfort with intellectual tension/discourse, self-confidence, coping skills when faced with failure, and ability to handle critique and constructive feedback (Olszewski-Kubilius, 2013).

Development of these psychosocial skills should be part of the climate of the classroom, discussed across every content area and modeled daily by the entire class or school community. Students can self-evaluate and make plans for improving and tracking their growth in these skills (see Chapter 9). One resource that can be used is Angela Duckworth's Grit Scale. A 12-item scale is available for adults as well as an 8-item scale for children (the site also has them in Chinese, French and German) can be found at this site: https://sites.sas.upenn.edu/duckworth/pages/research.

These scales give adults and students an idea of how "gritty" they are. If they have a low score, then they can make a conscious effort to improve their ability to bounce back after a less-than-successful performance or failure to master a new concept. They can begin working toward being diligent about their actions. Interviewing community and family members who showed perseverance and demonstrated grit throughout their lives is an assignment that can have a great impact on students.

Hand-in-hand with nurturing grit and resiliency is teaching students how to learn from errors and failure. Mistakes should be considered "data"—this data can help a student set goals for moving toward success.

A recommended first step in deliberate cultivation of psychosocial skills is to reflect upon what is already in place in your classroom or school. Focus on a few areas that overlap at first, such as perseverance, resiliency, and grit, and then gather some interested staff members. Together, brainstorm school or districtwide experiences that will deliberately cultivate these noncognitive factors. Establish "look fors" and a plan for monitoring student progress over time in the areas of concentration. Resource 1: Deliberate Cultivation of Psychosocial Skills (p. 5) can be helpful to you and your staff as you complete these tasks.

Building a Conceptual Understanding of the Brain and Neural Networks

Having an understanding of neural networking can significantly increase motivation. In Carol Dweck's (2010) original New York City study, students reported that visualizing neural connections helped them move forward. In my visits to schools, I have often heard students state that they think about the neurons connecting when they are faced with a difficult task or have difficulty understanding a new skill or concept. This does not require going deep into neuroscience, just building a conceptual understanding can increase motivation to succeed. Ideas for teaching students about neural networking can be found in *Mindsets in the Classroom* on pages 110–117 or in Chapter 8 of this book.

Growth Mindset Feedback and Praise

Strive for a learning space that praises effort, struggle, and perseverance. Provide feedback and praise when students select difficult tasks to conquer or try new strategies when learning a concept. This feedback also encompasses how you react to student behavior, such as a typically strong student not having success on an assessment. The learning environment, whether it is a classroom, field, court, in front of a piano, or at the kitchen table should be a setting where both adults and students favor the word "yet." "You are not quite there . . . yet . . . with more practice, you will be."

Two great video resources for growth mindset praise include:

⚙ *Carol Dweck: A Study on Praise and Mindsets presented by Trevor Ragan.* This is a great synthesis of Dweck's research on the impact of praise. It can be viewed at http://m.youtube.com/watch?feature=youtu.be&v=NWv1VdDeoRY

Deliberate Cultivation of Noncognitive Factors

School/Office/Program: _____   Date: _____

Psychosocial Skill	Actions Our School/District Has Already Taken to Cultivate These Skills	Ideas to Cultivate Noncognitive Factors	Ideas for Monitoring and Measuring Progress in This Area
Perseverance			
Grit			
Resiliency			
Learning From Failure			

Ready-to-Use Resources for Mindsets in the Classroom © Prufrock Press Inc.

✪ *Sesame Street: Janelle Monae—Power of Yet.* This Sesame Street video is a fun way to reinforce the importance of the word "yet." It can be viewed at https://www.youtube.com/watch?v=XLeUvZvuvAs

These four components, when implemented with integrity, will allow for an optimal growth mindset environment. Resource 2: Important Components in a Growth Mindset School Learning Environment (p. 7) serves as a reminder for teachers, and Resource 3: Classroom Poster (p. 8) can be hung in schools and classrooms as guidance for students. (To download a larger version of this poster and others in the book, please visit http://www.prufrock.com/assets/clientpages/mindset_resources.aspx.)

Important Components in a Growth Mindset Learning Environment

☑ Equitable access to advanced learning opportunities.

☑ Deliberate cultivation of psychosocial skills such as perseverance, resiliency, and grit.

☑ Student understanding of neural networks in the brain.

☑ Growth mindset feedback and praise.

Classroom Poster

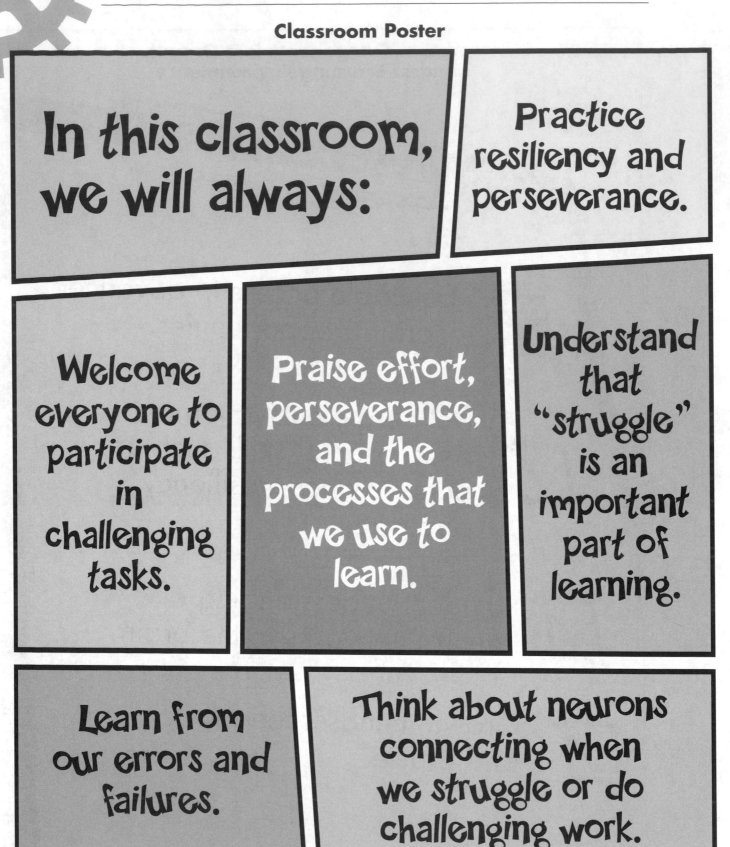

Ready-to-Use Resources for Mindsets in the Classroom © Prufrock Press Inc.

CHAPTER 2

WHAT ARE SOME WAYS TO BEGIN BUILDING A GROWTH MINDSET SCHOOL CULTURE?

Imperative to a growth mindset school culture is the understanding of the impact that an adult mindset has on our students. Fixed and growth mindset implications for achievement are an important discussion point for all adults working with children. If a teacher, parent, coach, or instructor of any kind possesses a fixed mindset regarding a child's ability, talent, or skills then the impact can have negative conscequences for the child.

Reflecting on present belief systems about intelligence is a good place to start with administrators, school staff, and high school students. Before any growth mindset professional learning takes place, ask participants to reflect on their present beliefs about intelligence. Using Resource 4: My Beliefs About Intelligence (p. 10), educators or students should consider what they have learned or observed about human intelligence. Make sure they know that this is a private document, for their own reflection. Later, after learning more about growth and fixed mindsets and neuroplasticity, they can do the task again and compare any changes in their belief system.

My Beliefs About Intelligence

Please share your beliefs about intelligence and/or what you were taught about student intelligence as you prepared to become a teacher.

My beliefs about intelligence are:

Upon completion, put this in an envelope and put your name and today's date on the front of the envelope.

Later in the year, open the envelope and look at the response you wrote today. Reflect on any changes in your response.

Note. From *Mindsets in the Classroom* (p. 15) by M. C. Ricci, 2013, Waco, TX: Prufrock Press. Copyright 2013 by Prufrock Press. Reprinted with permission.

Implications of Fixed and Growth Mindsets in the Classroom

When working with educators toward a growth mindset culture, it is important that they have an opportunity to discuss the potential implications of both a fixed and growth mindset. After preliminary learning about fixed and growth mindsets, Resource 5: Ways That Mindsets Influence Student Achievement (p. 12) can be used as a formative assessment prior to a professional learning session. It is a tool that will guide educators to self-reflect about implications for achievement and also serve as talking points in a larger discussion at the team level or for the entire staff.

Opportunities to Share Concerns

Early in the transition toward a growth mindset school or district culture, allow opportunities for staff to acknowledge potential or perceived barriers to establishing a growth mindset environment. Opportunities must occur that will allow educators to share concerns and openly express why they might believe that "this will never work" or think, "Here comes another initiative that everyone will forget about in 6 months." Providing opportunities to get these thoughts and concerns out in the open can help reduce the conversations behind the scenes, which have the potential to derail school or district goals. In order to get "buy-in" to a growth mindset philosophy, allow time for staff to express these thoughts, concerns, and feelings so that they can be addressed proactively and your learning community can move on toward established goals. One example of a perceived barrier that has come up often during my visits is the perception that this is "one more thing" that administrators are asking them to do. This is an easy one to address because a growth mindset is more of a philosophy than pedagogy. It is a way of thinking about our children and our self. It is not a new set of standards to learn, a kit to unpack and study, or a set of new instructional strategies . . . it is a way of thinking, a belief that one has about the potential and possibilities in our students.

On visits to several school districts, I asked teachers to identify potential or perceived barriers to a growth mindset school culture. The following is a sampling of items that were identified as potential barriers. On a side note, I facilitated these discussions with teachers without their administrators present. What is interesting is that some of the responses uncovered a great deal of fixed mindset thinking from the participants, which served as an effective preassessment for me; I discovered more about the mindsets of the educators I was working with. See if you can identify some of the fixed mindset thoughts in the lists below.

RESOURCE 5

Ways That Mindsets Influence Student Achievement

Ways that an educator's **fixed mindset** might influence student achievement and equitable access to advanced learning opportunities	Ways that an educator's **growth mindset** might influence student achievement and equitable access to advanced learning opportunities

Perceived Barriers to a Growth Mindset Environment

Responses From Elementary Teachers:

A growth mindset culture would be difficult in our district because . . .

- Outside factors (home life, parents, etc.)
- We can't allow kids to "fail" so that they can learn from it
- We don't want our students to struggle
- Our class size is too big
- We can't educate all of the teachers
- Our administrators will not "allow" teachers to stray from the curriculum to teach about growth mindset and brain lessons
- Many of our teachers have resistance to anything "new"
- We have teachers with a fixed mindset
- We need to educate the parents first
- Test scores and grades prevent a growth mindset

Responses From Middle School Teachers:

- Lack of parent support
- The high school has a fixed mindset
- Too many initiatives going on
- Language barriers (English language learners)
- Diverse learners (emotional issues)
- Kid perceptions
- Time
- Middle school kids give up easily
- Testing and grades

Responses From High School Teachers:

- Student buy-in: motivation
- No one will take responsibility for it
- State testing and grades prevent growth mindset thinking
- Kids are not intrinsically motivated
- Failure = F and F's are not OK
- Attendance
- Lack of consistency among teachers
- Teachers have fixed mindsets

Once these perceived barriers are on the table, discussions should take place that will proactively address these possible obstacles. Without addressing these obstacles in an open and constructive way, educators may have conversations behind the scenes that could actually hinder the process of creating a growth mindset environment.

Many of the groups I have worked with have mentioned that high-stakes test requirements and grading policies do not allow for a growth mindset environment.

This is one barrier I agree with to a certain extent. Test scores and grades focus on the end result, not the process, the effort, or the perseverance. We have many students who do not demonstrate their potential through a traditional assessment. The emphasis on testing trickles down from higher education. The good news is that we are seeing more and more colleges and universities going "test optional" (in some cases, interviews replace the test scores)—there is hope that this leads to a decreased emphasis on testing in K–12 as well. According to FairTest: The National Center for Fair and Open Testing, in 2014, more than 800 four-year colleges and universities did not use SAT and/or ACT scores as part of their application and acceptance processes.

Additionally, author and professor, Adam Grant wrote a spot-on opinion piece, "Throw Out the College Application System" for *The New York Times* in 2014 that suggests students attend an Assessment Center as part of the college application system rather than spending 5 hours on a Saturday morning taking the SAT or ACT. This center would have components that some would consider nontraditional. Grant suggested a combination of group activities, interviews, and measures of creativity. I would add that tasks could also be in place where noncognitive factors such as perseverance, work ethic, and grit could be observed. Yes, I know, we are not there yet . . . but there is hope.

What schools and districts do have control over is grading policies and reporting procedures. Look at your present grading and reporting system through a growth mindset lens. Do you see these words/phrases: *perseverance, resilience,* or *work ethic*? Is there somewhere to comment, rate, or report progress on a student's learning processes and willingness to learn from errors? We are living in an era of high-stakes state testing (e.g., PARCC, Smarter Balance, or state-developed assessments), and in general, we as individual teachers, schools, and districts cannot change or opt out of these assessments. However, we do have control over grading and report cards. As this will most likely be mentioned by educators in your school or district as a barrier to a growth mindset environment, I urge you to acknowledge what cannot be changed yet (e.g., state testing) and focus on what can be changed, refined, or adjusted (e.g., grading and reporting).

Finally, another perceived barrier has been brought up many times during this exercise, "What about the teacher who has a fixed mindset but thinks he has a growth mindset?" This is one of the reasons that growth mindset needs to be revisited throughout the year(s). As educators become engaged in their learning, provide continual opportunities for self-reflection and use role-playing as another way for them to discover some areas of fixed mindset thinking.

Resource 6: Perceived and Potential Barriers Toward a Growth Mindset Environment (p. 15) provides a template for educators to get all of those things that they might be thinking down on paper, as well as a way for them to brainstorm possible solutions for addressing the barriers they face. Ask the group to reflect on potential barriers individually or with a partner and then open the discussion with

Perceived and Potential Barriers
Toward a Growth Mindset Environment

Possible Barrier	Proactive Plan to Address Barrier

the larger group. This is not something to rush through. Plan for plenty of time and, in some instances, more than one session. This is an important step to ensure teacher commitment. As you revisit growth mindset throughout the school year, refer back to the barriers list and eliminate them as needed.

Recognizing Fixed and Growth Mindset Words and Actions

Evaluation of video clips from movies is another way to view fixed and growth mindsets in a variety of situations. The Observation of Fixed and Growth Mindset form in Resource 7 (p. 17) is a simple, yet effective way to ask both adults and students to view a clip and observe the characters' words and actions. As educators or students view the film clip, they will look for evidence of both fixed and growth mindsets.

One of my favorite clips to use is the Chris Gardner interview clip in *The Pursuit of Happyness* (Alper, Clayman, D'Esposito, Zee, & Muccino, 2006; see https://www.youtube.com/watch?v=gHXKitKAT1E). In this scene, many of the gentlemen around the table who are participating in the interview demonstrate fixed mindset actions from the beginning; no eye contact when shaking hands, facial expressions, etc. Conversely, Chris Gardner demonstrates growth mindset thinking through his words and actions, for example, when he references not knowing something he strongly states, "I will find the answer." A variety of other video clips for viewing fixed and growth mindset can be found in Figure 1.

After viewing the chosen video clip, discuss what was observed with the group. Some discussion may occur regarding the interpretation of what was seen. This exercise can open the eyes of all who are participating and allow self-reflection—particularly in the area of nonverbal actions that could inadvertently be sending a fixed mindset message. I also like to use this exercise as a formative assessment for both teachers and students.

Fixed Mindset Practices

Monitoring and reviewing progress toward a growth mindset environment is as important as building one. Chapter 9 will offer a resource focused on what to "Look For" as you build your growth mindset environment. However, we need to take a fresh look around our schools in order to identify fixed mindset thinking.

Observation of Fixed and Growth Mindset

Character	Fixed Mindset Statements and Actions	Growth Mindset Statements and Actions	Other Observations

- Kathy Bates as Miss Sue in *The Blind Side* (Hancock, 2009) https://www.youtube.com/watch?v=38Xuz-r8Q5U&feature=youtu.be& list=PLfM-YfRN00toPuUcmpGa2avMI6QOYtbUi

- Surf scout scene in *Surf's Up* (Brannon & Buck 2007) http://www.wingclips.com/movie-clips/surfs-up/surf-scout

- Wonders of science in *Cloudy With a Chance of Meatballs 2* (Cameron & Pearn, 2013) http://www.wingclips.com/movie-clips/cloudy-with-a-chance-of-meatballs -2/wonders-of-science

- Test launches in *October Sky* (Johnston, 1999; this is a good one for students to observe resiliency) https://www.youtube.com/watch?v=cP_OM5VVcSo

FIGURE 1. A FEW OPTIONS FOR OBSERVING FIXED AND GROWTH MINDSET.

When I visit schools now, I notice things that I would have previously overlooked when I was a classroom teacher. I always make a point to look around and see what is lining the halls and classrooms. Something that can be overlooked in schools trying to build a growth mindset culture is the fixed mindset displays and bulletin boards. For example, in one elementary school, I saw a bulletin board that had big letters saying "Top Dog" on it. I noticed that student papers that were displayed were, for the most part, neat and correct. What message does this send about the value of struggle, errors, and failure? How might the phrase "Top Dog" be interpreted by students?

At the elementary level, I have noticed lots of charts displaying stickers for students who have mastered basic facts in a given time period—note that just the students who have mastery are recognized with a sticker. I saw no stickers for showing improvement or growth in basic facts. By the way, what about those stickers? Take a look at what some of those stickers that we use in the classroom say: "Perfect!", "100%", "A+". Throw those away and find stickers that celebrate effort, growth, or progress. Instead of giving parents bumper stickers that read "My son is an honor roll student at Chestnut Hill Elementary School" why not say, "My son demonstrates perseverance at Chestnut Hill Elementary School" or "My daughter puts forth great effort at Chestnut Hill Elementary School"?

Reflect on your school celebrations as well. Several educators have asked about the value of the often-used honor roll assembly. One educator in Colorado explained to me that in her school they hold these assemblies quarterly and the same kids are always sitting in the back two rows—those who are never recognized. If this is an event that you hold in your school or district, then gather your leadership team together and ask them what the purpose of this event is. If the response is to recognize good grades, I would argue that the "reward" was the grade. (On a side note—

some of the A's were made without a whole lot of effort from the students; they were underchallenged.) If the response is to motivate others, then, take note, are the same students being unrecognized every time? Is this assembly really motivating others? If this is an event that can't possibly be eliminated due to outside pressure, then use the time to celebrate growth and hard work rather than grades.

Look at all of your school practices through a growth mindset lens (see Resource 53 later in this book). Challenge your staff to do the same and you may be surprised about what you see.

CHAPTER 3

WHY IS A DIFFERENTIATED, RESPONSIVE CLASSROOM IMPORTANT TO A GROWTH MINDSET CULTURE?

Responsive instruction is about meeting students where they are when they walk through your classroom door. It is about focusing on students' unmet needs at the beginning of an instructional sequence rather then waiting until the middle or end. Differentiated, responsive instruction must occur as part of a teacher's daily routine. Resource 8: Teacher Checklist for Planning Differentiated, Responsive Instruction (p. 22) provides suggested guidelines for planning a responsive instructional unit. (It has been tweaked from the original checklist that is on page 54 of *Mindsets in the Classroom*.) This resource can help guide teachers in planning a responsive unit. See Chapter 3 in *Mindsets in the Classroom* for more details.

This is just one model for differentiated, responsive instruction. It doesn't matter what model you use as long as all students have equitable opportunities to grow without academic ceilings or relying on a child's testing or label (LD, GT, TAG, advanced, etc.) in order to have their instructional needs met. Children should not have to jump through hoops to gain access to enriched, advanced, or accelerated learning experiences. If there is a precedence for not allowing students to engage in above-grade-level standards, think about this: If a standard states that the students must be able to count to 10 and a child can count to 20, do you say "Oh, I'm sorry, but according to our grade-level standards, you are not allowed to count to 20 until next year"? We would never limit a child in this situation, so why is it that some schools and districts don't "allow" students to accelerate to above-grade-level standards?

Equitable access to advanced instruction can occur more successfully when educators are given the tools and the time to informally or formally assess where students are at any given point in time. Educators must also be committed to seeking out and spotting potential and talent in students who may not demonstrate strengths in a traditional manner.

Teacher Checklist for Planning Differentiated, Responsive Instruction

❑ Determine skills, content, concepts, or procedures being assessed and develop or use school/district preassessments.

❑ Develop anchor activities related to the unit.

❑ Present preview (2–5 minutes) to activate background knowledge prior to preassessment.

❑ Students take preassessment.

❑ Analyze preassessment: determine areas already mastered, any gaps that may exist, and areas of need for each student.

❑ Identify students who would benefit from curriculum compacting and plan instruction for the areas of need.

❑ Identify any students who have complete understanding and are ready for another learning outcome. Plan for enrichment and topic/content acceleration for these students.

❑ Form instructional groups—model anchor activity expectations if necessary and share the group rotation for the day. Teacher will instruct each group every day. Plan for a few minutes between groups to respond to any questions from students, make sure everyone is on the right track, and praise effort students are putting forth.

❑ Administer formative assessment daily. Use the information to inform instruction for students as well reflection for the teacher. If understanding is not evident with most students, reteach in a new way. Student movement among groups may occur based on the formative assessments.

❑ Summative assessments, performance tasks, and products (as well as homework) must be differentiated based on the instruction for each group.

Note. Adapted from *Mindsets in the Classroom* (p. 54) by M. C. Ricci, 2013, Waco, TX: Prufrock Press. Copyright 2013 by Prufrock Press. Adapted with permission.

Preassessments

In order to be responsive, we need to figure out where students are at the beginning of an instructional sequence. We do this through routine use of preassessments with previewing. The effective use of preassessment is essential to ensuring that students and teachers both work from a growth mindset, believing that effort and perseverance are the most important attributes that determine success. Without preassessment, some students are not provided with opportunities to build resiliency, because they are never challenged or never have to struggle with learning. Even though formative assessments can be used to help determine differentiation needs during the course of instruction, preassessments allow for front-end differentiation.

Front-end differentiation allows teachers to plan for valuable enrichment and can also provide an opportunity for students to accelerate within the content topic at the beginning of a learning sequence. Preassessment respects a student's time and prior knowledge.

Previewing

Before jumping into developing your own or using a ready-made preassessment, an important precursor must take place. You must allow students the opportunity to first "preview" the content being assessed. Previewing primes the brain by stimulating memory in the area being assessed. I know what some of you are thinking: "If I do that, it will be too easy" or "That's cheating!" Not so. In fact, previewing provides an opportunity for students to activate background knowledge and previous learning prior to a preassessment so that the results will be a better reflection of what they understand.

Developing Preassessments

Deciding what kind of preassessment to use depends upon the content being assessed. Preassessments are not always paper-and-pencil tests. In the primary grades, you might ask students to demonstrate their knowledge using concrete math manipulatives or by conducting a structured discussion capturing understanding with anecdotal records or from the teacher's notes. If you want to assess their knowledge of measurement, then hand them a ruler and see what they can do. In trying to have students recognize the author's point of view, a teacher may meet with small groups and, through a guided discussion, note ideas related to understanding the concept. In both of these cases, teachers should keep observational records that capture evidence of student understanding at a range of levels from concrete to more abstract. Resource 9: Checklist for Developing Previews and Preassessments (pp. 24–25) provides a checklist that can be used as guidance when developing preassessments.

RESOURCE 9

Checklist for Developing Previews and Preassessments

❑ Preassessment preview: In order to prime the brain for the preassessment, select a 3–5 minute task that will activate background knowledge about the content being assessed. (This is not a lesson.) Some ideas for a preassessment preview: BrainPOP or other short video that reviews/introduces the content, a short text with a few focused questions guided by the teacher, a photograph or painting about the content, a few samples of the skill projected and discussed, a class discussion.

❑ A preassessment does *not* have to be a test or quiz. An example of a non-quiz format is included in the box below.

> This preassessment is designed to assess students' understanding of Common Core State Standard RL 4.3-Describe in depth a character, setting, or event in a story or drama, drawing on specific details in the text (e.g. a character's thoughts, words, or actions).
>
> 1. Choose a short text that has details about a character, setting, and event. Ask students to read it independently.
> 2. Ask students to write a summary of the text.
> 3. Students will then hear the story being read out loud by the teacher and follow along.
> 4. Students will then participate in a Shared Inquiry discussion using the text as a resource (see http://www.juniorgreatbooks.org for information about Shared Inquiry).
> 5. After the discussion, they may revise their original summary response.
> 6. The teacher will determine students' understanding of CCSS RL 4.3 through both their written response and their responses to the questions during the Shared Inquiry discussion. This provides two different opportunities for the student to demonstrate understanding—written and oral.

❑ The preassessment must measure understanding only in the standard/unit that is specifically being assessed. (You would not consider spelling, grammar, sentence structure, etc., for the above sample of CCSS RL 4.3.)

Checklist for Developing Previews and Preassessments, *continued*

❑ Teachers should read the preassessment directions out loud so all students understand what is being asked. (A struggling reader should not be penalized in math because he or she cannot read the directions.)

❑ Include a few sentences for teachers to read to students prior to the preassessment. This will help frame the reason for the preassessment, such as: "Today I want to see what you know about fractions. This task will not count as a grade but it is very important for you to do your best. This will help me plan instruction that is just right for you."

❑ Go deep. A math preassessment is not just computation, but should include application of the mathematical skill or concept. A preassessment measuring understanding of literary devices should ask students to not only identify them, but also to craft them.

❑ When developing a preassessment, use different formats, allowing students to demonstrate understanding from solving a problem to developing a problem. Avoid true/false, multiple choice, and other formats where a student can guess an answer.

❑ Assess each standard, skill, or concept in at least two ways.

❑ Include above-grade-level standards within the same topic. Some students will have mastery beyond their grade level.

❑ Analyze assessment results. Identify areas of mastery/understanding as well as any gaps in their learning. Compact curriculum for students who demonstrate understanding—this will allow for enrichment and acceleration for these students.

Formative Assessments

Use formative assessments (checking for understanding) daily. Don't grade them—use them to inform instruction. This can include ways to determine who needs reteaching (in a new way) and who is ready to move forward. Implement formative assessments in a variety of ways and let students know your goal when using them. Allow students to reflect on their learning and to identify their own learning goals. Resource 10: Formative Assessment for Learning About the Brain (p. 27) and Resource 11: Formative Assessment for Learning About Growth Mindset (p. 28) provide a way for students to think about what they have learned, to form questions, and to determine what they want to learn more about—which can become an individual learning goal for each student.

A wide variety of digital formative assessments have surfaced over the last few years. A good list can be found on the Common Sense Media website: https://www.graphite.org/top-picks/top-tech-tools-for-formative-assessment. Edutopia also provides a list of 53 Ways to Check for Understanding that can be found here: http://www.edutopia.org/pdfs/blogs/edutopia-finley-53ways-check-for-understanding.pdf.

The Frayer Model (Frayer, Frederick, & Klausmeier, 1969) is a visual organizer that can provide a more in-depth way to check for understanding. For example, if you are deliberately cultivating the concept of perseverance in your classroom, then you might use a Frayer Model that requires students to define perseverance, determine characteristics, and provide examples and nonexamples of perseverance. This will allow an educator more insight into the depth of their understanding. The blank Frayer Model in Resource 12 (p. 29) could be used to check for understanding of many mindset related concepts such as perseverance, resiliency, failure, grit, fixed mindset, and growth mindset. (Lots of other blank Frayer Model templates can be found online.) Allow students to use words, diagrams, or pictures to communicate their thoughts in each quadrant. Figure 2 includes some examples of Frayer Model formative assessments used by the Primary Talent Development teachers in Frederick County, MD.

Planning Templates

A planning template can be a helpful visual tool for new teachers, teachers just starting down the differentiation path, or experienced teachers who would like to use a visual or template for their planning. Resource 13: Differentiated/Responsive Teaching Template for Two Groups (p. 31) and Resource 14: Differentiated/Responsive Teaching for Three Groups (p. 32) provide planning templates that can be used to help teachers visualize what it means to be responsive to student needs. One guides teachers in thinking through a two-group responsive model and the other through a three-group responsive model.

Formative Assessment for Learning About the Brain

Learning About the Brain

3 Things I learned about the brain:

2 Things I have a question about:

1 Thing about the brain that I want to learn more about:

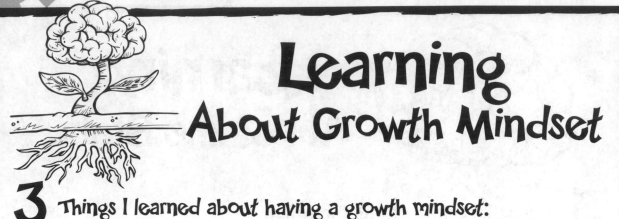

Learning
About Growth Mindset

3 Things I learned about having a growth mindset:

2 Things I have a question about:

1 Thing about having a growth mindset that I want to learn more about:

Blank Frayer Model

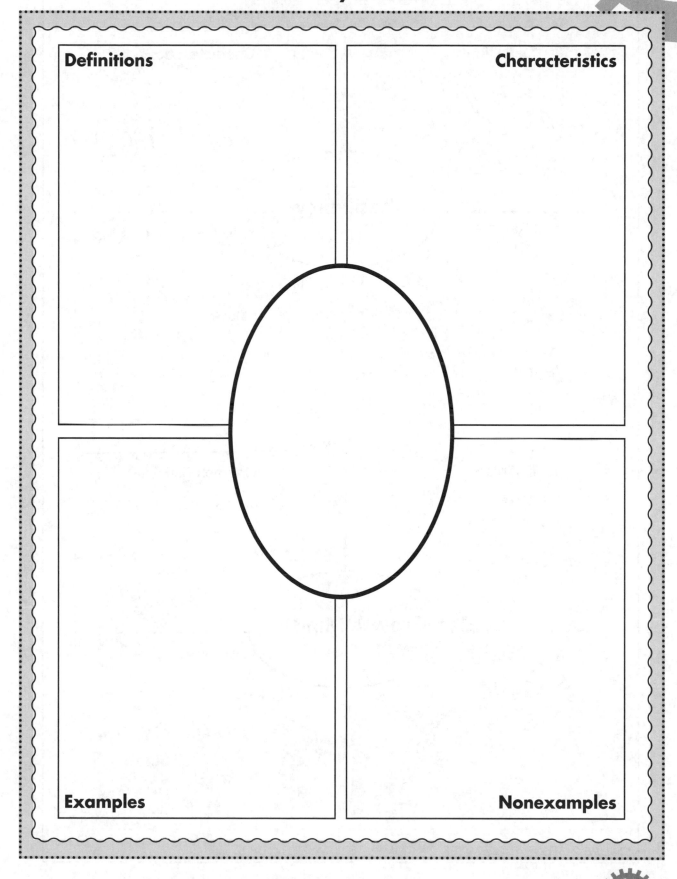

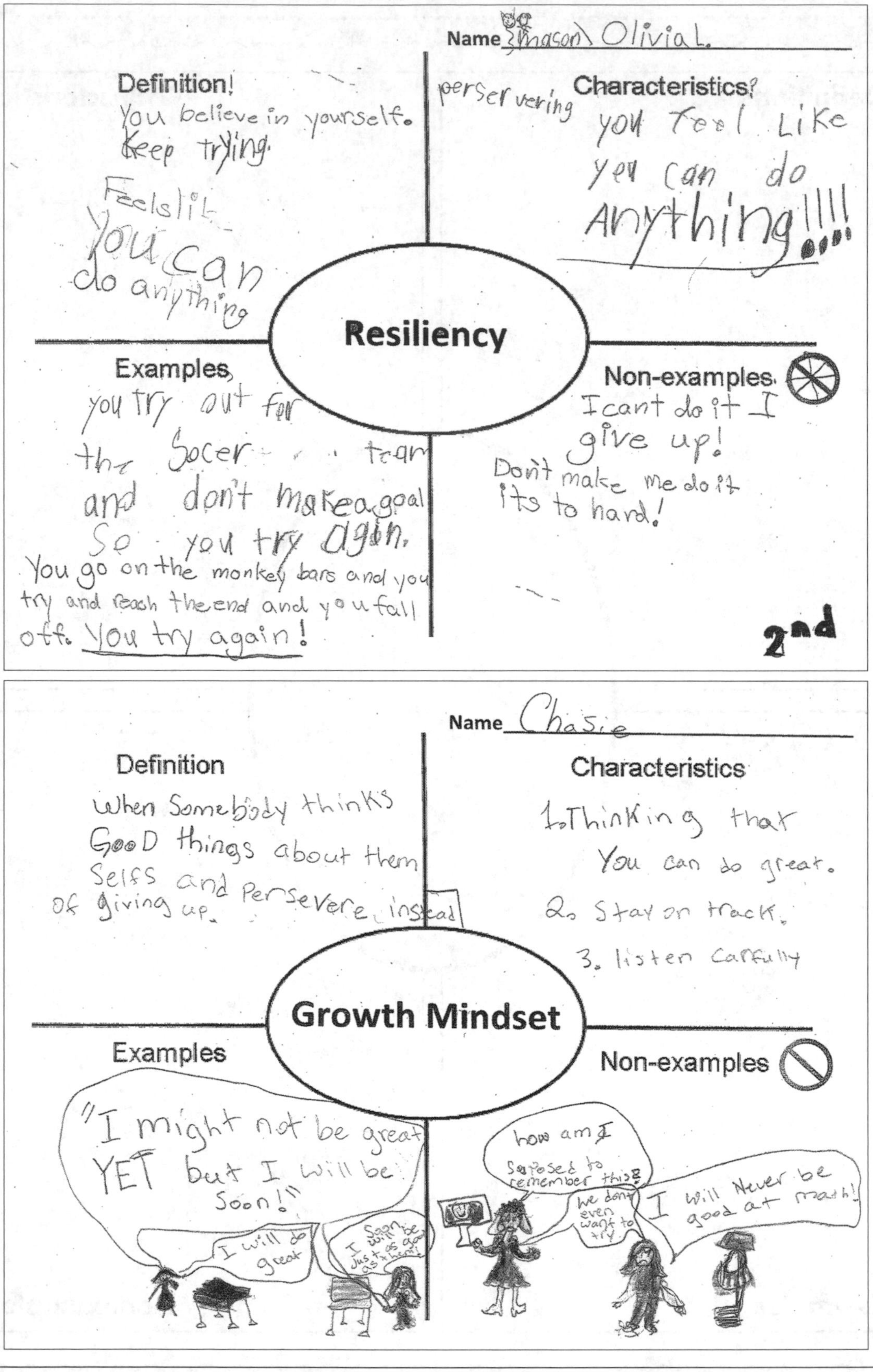

Name (Mason) Olivia L.

Definition!
You believe in yourself.
Keep trying.

Feels lik
you can
do anything

perservering **Characteristics?**
you Feel Like
you can do
ANything!!!!

Resiliency

Examples
you try out for
the Socer team
and don't make a goal
So you try agin.
You go on the monkey bars and you
try and reach the end and you fall
off. You try again!

Non-examples
I cant do it I
give up!
Don't make me do it
its to hard!

2nd

Name Chasie

Definition
When Somebody thinks
GooD things about them
Selfs and Persevere, instead
of giving up.

Characteristics
1. Thinking that
You can do great.
2. Stay on track.
3. listen Carfully

Growth Mindset

Examples

"I might not be great
YET but I will be
Soon!"

I will do
great

I sagn be
Just as good
as I want

Non-examples

how am I
saposed to
remember this?

we dont
even
want to
try

I will Never be
good at math!

FIGURE 2. STUDENT EXAMPLES OF COMPLETED FRAYER MODELS.

Differentiated/Responsive Teaching Template for Two Groups

Common Core State Standard Skill and/or Instructional Objective:

Preview and Preassessment

STOP

Preassessment must occur before planning differentiated groups

Whole Class Mini-Lesson: 5–15 minutes (optional)

Compacting (Include Instruction)

✂ Formative Assessments

Acceleration and/or Enrichment

Summative Assessment

Direct Instruction

⚓ Anchor Activities

Summative Assessment

Note. Adapted from *Mindsets in the Classroom* (p. 53) by M. C. Ricci, 2013, Waco, TX: Prufrock Press. Copyright 2013 by Prufrock Press. Adapted with permission.

Ready-to-Use Resources for Mindsets in the Classroom © Prufrock Press Inc.

Differentiated/Responsive Teaching Template for Three Groups

Common Core State Standard Skill and/or Instructional Objective:

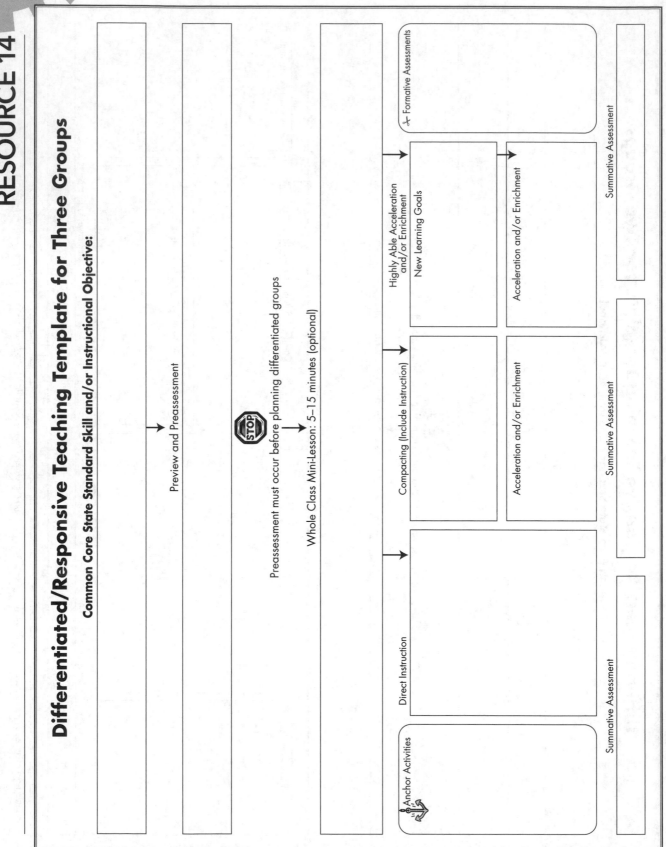

Preview and Preassessment

Preassessment must occur before planning differentiated groups

Whole Class Mini-Lesson: 5–15 minutes (optional)

Direct Instruction

Compacting (Include Instruction)

Highly Able Acceleration and/or Enrichment

New Learning Goals

Acceleration and/or Enrichment

Acceleration and/or Enrichment

⚓ Anchor Activities

⚓ Formative Assessments

Summative Assessment

Summative Assessment

Summative Assessment

Ready-to-Use Resources for Mindsets in the Classroom © Prufrock Press Inc.

WHY IS CRITICAL THINKING IMPORTANT IN A GROWTH MINDSET CLASS CULTURE?

Chapter 4 in *Mindsets in the Classroom* emphasized the importance of critical thinking learning opportunities for all students as part of a growth mindset environment. The Critical Thinking Growth Mindset Project shared in *Mindsets in the Classroom* resulted in teachers raising expectations for students who were not yet achieving at grade level, but flourished in critical thinking opportunities. Through critical thinking games, teachers were able to observe students who typically may not be given the opportunity to demonstrate their developing cognitive abilities. Because the teachers had already played the games during a workshop (and many were challenged as evidenced by a few game pieces being tossed across the table), they were impressed with the level of success that the children demonstrated and it altered the expectations for these students. In addition to the critical thinking games that were used in the project, teachers were also taught the critical reasoning exemplars that are shared in this chapter. The critical reasoning opportunities not only served as a great neural workout for the students but also served as a catalyst toward higher teacher expectations.

All students must have daily opportunities to think critically. The following strategies can be viewed as a menu—consider the standard that is being taught and determine if any of these strategies could be used to preview or preassess the content, teach the standard, check for understanding, enrich the learning, build a conceptual understanding, or review or assess the standard.

Feed-BACK

A critical thinking exemplar that builds on lessons learned from Jerome Bruner's (1961) Concept Attainment Model is a critical thinking strategy that I call "Feed-BACK." It is a strategy that helps students develop processes needed for deductive reasoning.

Feed-BACK was inspired by a vintage cocktail party game, bumping up the game play so that critical reasoning is required. As a child, when my parents had a party (and I spied from upstairs), each party guest who entered the house had a sticker placed on his or her back with the name of a person who was half of a popular couple or celebrity at the time: Barbie and Ken, Lucy and Ricky, Diana Ross, Marvin Gaye, etc. The guests were charged with trying to figure out the name on their back by asking questions of the other guests.

Feed-BACK takes it further—students are given the name of a person, a number, a geographic location, or an object on a sticker on their back and they must determine who or what is on their back by asking only questions that can be answered with a yes or a no. Resource 15: Feed-BACK Directions (p. 36) includes the steps for this critical reasoning strategy and Resource 16: Feed-BACK Labels (p. 37) provides a sample set that will enrich and extend the conversation about growth mindset. The people listed on the sample set are people who have overcome adversity, demonstrated resiliency and grit, experienced failure, and/or demonstrated a growth mindset. This sample set is recommended for grades 4–12, however I have used the Feed-BACK strategy beginning with kindergarten students—with modeling and sometimes sentence stems. For younger students, the stickers on their backs could have numbers, shapes, pictures of story characters, etc.

At the end of or during the debriefing process, teachers may also introduce or reinforce the concept of deductive reasoning by asking the students what kind of questions they asked at the beginning of the process. Most students begin with more general questions: "Is my character a girl?" or "Am I alive?" As they learn more about their character or word, questions become more specific.

Concept Placemats

Concept placemats use images that share a common attribute to guide students toward developing a concept. Is there a concept that you are teaching that students may be able to develop more deeply using images? This strategy allows students to generate many possibilities about sets of images and it is structured so that students have to first look at pairs of objects to find many different common concepts, then groups of three until they may look at every image together. Take a look at Resource

17: Concept Placement for Concept of Three (p. 38), created for kindergarten or first-grade students. After asking the students for two images that share a common concept, some of the responses might include:

⊛ The bike and the magic genie lamp. They are both metal.

⊛ The clover and the genie lamp. They both give wishes/good luck/are magic.

⊛ The hen and the pig. They both can be found on a farm.

⊛ The binder and the circus. They both have three circles.

After asking for three things that share a common concept, student responses might include:

⊛ The hen, the pig, and the elephant. They are all animals/they all have feet.

⊛ The three-leaf clover, the bike, and the circus. They are all found on the ground.

At some point during this exercise, ask the students to really look at the details in each image. Pose questions such as: Why is the hen wearing a hat? Why does the hen have a mustache? I wonder where this hen lives. (Is it a French hen?)

Ask students to think about all of the connections that they have made so far and think of a common concept among all of the images. If someone comes up with the concept of three, ask for an explanation of the student's thinking. For example, you might hear:

⊛ The pig is part of the Three Little Pigs.

⊛ The bike has three wheels.

⊛ The clover has three leaves.

⊛ The hen is part of three French hens.

⊛ The binder has three rings.

⊛ The genie lamp will grant three wishes.

If no one comes up with the concept you developed, acknowledge any other concepts that work and invite the students to think about it during the day so that it can be revisited the next day. You can also add an additional image such as a birthday cake with three candles.

This can be projected on a Smart Board or each student can have his or her own placemat. Resource 18: Concept Placemats: A Step-by-Step Guide for Teachers (p. 39) provides directions about how to develop a concept placemat. Two additional Concept Placemat samples for older students are also provided. In Resource 19 (p. 40), the concept being developed is growth, and in Resource 20 (p. 41), the concept being developed is resiliency.

RESOURCE 15

Feed-BACK Directions

Directions

➢ Each student will have the name of a famous (or semi-famous) character/person on their back. The challenge is to figure out who is there.

➢ Each student may ask questions that can be answered with a "yes" or a "no." They may ask another student up to two questions, then move on to someone else.

➢ If students want to, they may use paper and pencil to write down what they have learned.

➢ If someone asks a question about the person on their back, and the student answering is not sure of an answer, they should say that they do not know. (Instead of giving incorrect information.)

➢ As each student goes through the process of solving the mystery of who is on their back, they should be aware of the kind of thinking that they are using.

➢ At the end of the given time, (when at least half know who they are) gather students together and discuss the process. Ask the students who do not know yet to keep the sticker on their back because the group may be able to suggest additional questions for them to ask.

➢ Begin a discussion by asking the following: By show of hands ask: How many of you know who is on your back? How many can describe the person, but cannot think of the specific name? Who needs some ideas about what questions they can ask next?

Debrief the Process

➢ Did anyone have a specific strategy that you used? Explain.

➢ What was the most valuable question that you asked?

➢ In addition to asking the questions, did anything else help you?

➢ What kind of thinking did you do?

➢ Is there anything that you would have done differently?

Feed-BACK Labels

People Who Have Overcome Adversity, Demonstrated Resiliency and Perseverance, Learned From Setbacks, and/or Demonstrated a Growth Mindset

Write the names of these people on blank labels and carefully place a label on each student's back so that they cannot see the name. Choose names that are best suited to the age group. After the strategy, students may then research what each person has overcome, what setback he or she has had in life, and ways he or she persevered and demonstrated a growth mindset.

Jim Carrey	Sidney Poitier
Stevie Wonder	Harrison Ford
Demi Lovato	The Beatles
Bethany Hamilton	James Dyson (vacuum)
Elvis Presley	Vincent Van Gogh
Halle Berry	Agatha Christie
Vera Wang	Lucille Ball
Jennifer Lopez	Ulysses S. Grant
Jay-Z	Abraham Lincoln
Bill Gates	Eminem
Ed Sheeran	Martha Stewart
Simon Cowell	R. H. Macy
Thomas Edison	Colonel Sanders
Michael Jordan	Steven Spielberg
Oprah Winfrey	Mark Cuban
Dr. Seuss	Charles Darwin
J. K. Rowling	Louisa May Alcott
Beethoven	Jack London
Babe Ruth	Fred Astaire
John Grisham	Steve Jobs
Soichiro Honda (car maker)	Nelson Mandela

Concept Placemat

Find pairs of objects that share a common concept.

Find 3 objects that share a common concept.

What concept do all of these images have in common?

Be prepared to tell why.

Concept Placemats:
A Step-by-Step Guide for Teachers

Concept formation relates to making connections, seeing relationships between items of information, and defining a concept from them. Concept formation is a key skill required for learning of new ideas.

Is there a concept based on a content area that is being studied that you would like your students to form using images? Choosing a more abstract concept works best. For example, "relationships" works better than "pets."

➢ Once you choose a concept, brainstorm ideas about what kinds of images might represent that particular concept.

➢ Develop the concept placemat with the computer, open a document, and add images. Insert pictures using clip art or images found online (three to six images are usually enough to build a concept).

➢ The placemat can be projected or each student can have a copy of the placemat.

Using the Placemat

Within an instructional sequence, determine how the placemat will be used: As a pre or formative assessment? Activator? A vehicle for learning new information? A springboard to a discussion? To enrich and extend a concept? Something else?

Ask students to look at the placemat quietly. Give everyone a set time (1–2 minutes), then ask for ideas (otherwise the "quick thinkers" dominate) using questions similar to these:

➢ Who can find two things that are the same in some way? (Take all student responses. During this time, observe/listen for unique connections between the images.)

➢ Who can find three things that are the same in some way? (Take all student responses. During this time, observe/listen for unique connections between the images.)

➢ Let's look for some things that are the same among all of the images. (Take all student responses. During this time, observe/listen for unique connections between the images.)

➢ Let's hear some ideas for adding more things that also share the same concept.

➢ Let's think about why I might have chosen this concept for our class. What do you think we will be talking about? What do you think we are going to learn about? (This question should ask about the content connection of the strategy).

➢ Any ideas for adding an additional image that shares the same concept?

Note. Adapted from *Mindsets in the Classroom* (pp. 129–131) by M. C. Ricci, 2013, Waco, TX: Prufrock Press. Copyright 2013 by Prufrock Press. Adapted with permission.

Concept Placemat

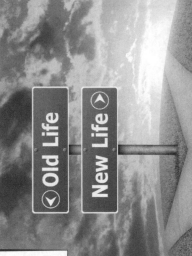

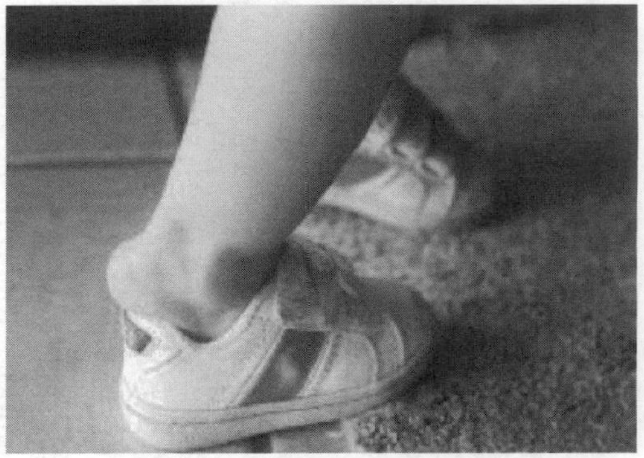

Find pairs of objects that share a common concept.

Find 3 objects that share a common concept.

What concept do all of these images have in common?

Be prepared to tell why.

Ready-to-Use Resources for Mindsets in the Classroom © Prufrock Press Inc.

Concept Placemat

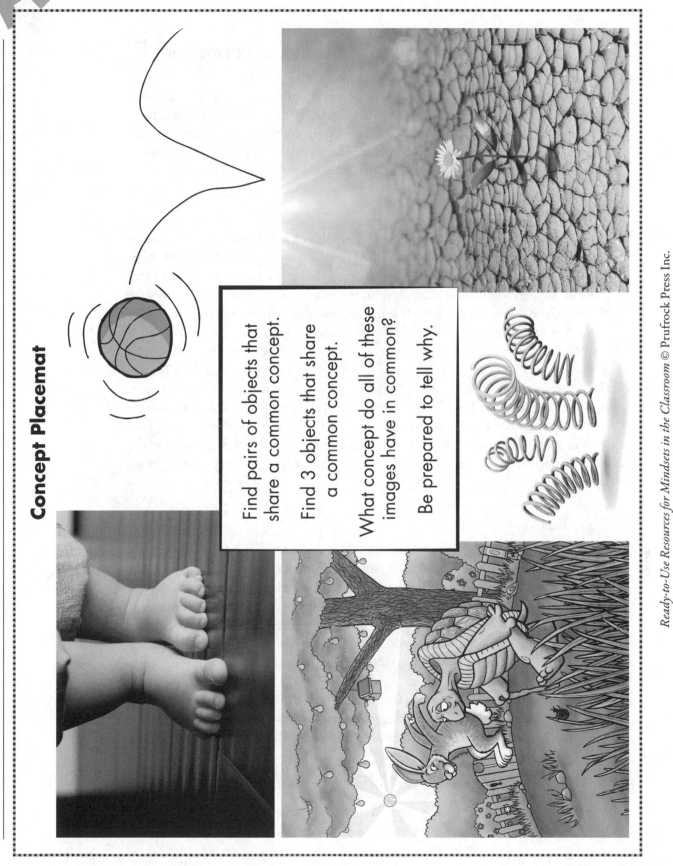

Find pairs of objects that share a common concept.

Find 3 objects that share a common concept.

What concept do all of these images have in common?

Be prepared to tell why.

Concept Development and Concept Formation

The following resources give more detail for two of the strategies that are mentioned in *Mindsets in the Classroom*: Guess Box (pp. 107–109) and Collections (pp.120–122) These two strategies are adapted from exemplars that were originally created for Montgomery County Public Schools, MD, Program of Assessment, Diagnosis and Instruction (PADI) that was in existence through 2012.

Guess Box

Like Feed-BACK, the Guess Box strategy builds on lessons learned from Jerome Bruner's Concept Attainment Model. The Guess Box strategy requires students to determine what item is in a box (the item is chosen because it relates to a content area in some way). A box in which the contents are unknown can be a powerful tool for thinking, and it is very important that the facilitator not end the Guess Box activity at the first indication that students know what is in the box.

Students must determine what is in the box by asking only questions that can be answered with a yes or a no. Resource 21 (p. 44) includes the directions for the Guess Box strategy, and Resource 22 (p. 46) provides some growth mindset ideas for items to put in the box. A Guess Box can feel clumsy the first few times you do it, so persevere! After you and your students go through a few of them, you will see growth in the way students ask questions and reason. You will also see growth in the way you determine clues and respond to questions that do not clearly have yes or no answers.

Collections

A collection of objects assembled around a specific concept can be used to help students develop classification skills, analyze attributes of objects, discover relationships between items, and form a concept. There are two kinds of collections, **serial** and **revealed**. In a revealed collection, all objects are displayed at the same time. If the common link between the objects is obvious, a revealed collection works well. Focus would be on finding subcategories and contrast within the group. A set of toy animals or models of transportation that share a connection would make an appropriate revealed collection.

A serial collection is used when items are displayed one at a time. The collection should not be formed around anything to do with words such as things that begin with a "B" or "compound words." It is about the attributes of the items that require deep critical thought.

The order of each item revealed is very purposeful. After each item, the teacher records students' predictions on index cards or sticky notes as to what the collection may be focused on. After each item is revealed, the teacher reviews all of the predictions that have already been generated. Students determine if the card/sticky note

Guess Box Directions

A box in which the contents are unknown can be a powerful tool for thinking. The item in a Guess Box should be chosen because of how it relates to a content area. It can be also used as a pre- or formative assessment. Prior to the lesson, set up two columns on the board or chart paper. At the top of one column, write "Attributes of a _____". At the top of the second column (this column can be small) put a "?".

First, tell the students that you have something in the box and their job is to find out what is in it. They may only ask questions that can be answered with a "yes" or "no." The "no" answers are just as important as the "yes" answers because they give us very valuable information about what is in the box.

On the chart paper, record the "positive attributes" that are learned through the questions. (Don't list "not yellow," "not round" etc.) At the end of the strategy, a list of words and phrases that describe the item in the box will be already charted for the students to use.

There is no limit as to how many questions can be asked. In fact, when many of the students know what is in the box is when the questioning becomes higher level and the teacher recognizes "sparks" in his or her students.

Guess Box Guidelines

➢ Be sure to tell the students if you have the real thing in the box or a model/picture of the real thing. (With a model/picture, questions are asked/answered as if it is the real thing.)

➢ Have a few clues ready if you need them. Always begin with one clue before the questioning begins. If the group is small, be more generous with your clue.

    O The clue should have *nothing* to do with the word. For example, if you had a pumpkin in the box, you would never say: "It begins with a P." The word has nothing to do with the attributes of the object.

➢ Only record the positive attribute (the "yes" answers).

    O Example: edible, fruit, round, orange, white, green, seeds, grows on a vine, can be carved, see them mostly in the fall, grows in a patch, has pulp, turned into a carriage in a fairy tale, some are too heavy to carry, you can cook the seeds

➢ If students ask, "Is it big? Soft? Heavy?" and so on, ask them to compare it to something by saying, "As heavy as what?" or "As soft as what?"

➢ Occasionally a question is asked that the teacher cannot answer or feels that the answer would mislead the students. In this case, write the question under the "?" column to discuss with students after the object is revealed.

➢ When it appears that some students have a good idea about what might be in the box, ask them, "How many of you can come up with three (or two) new questions that I can answer 'yes' to?" (This requires students to think more critically about what it is the box.)

➢ Most teachers end a Guess Box too soon. When it appears that most kids know what is in the box, keep going to see who can come up with more in-depth questions. (Observe who is asking higher level questions.)

➢ When it appears that the students know what is in the box, say "1-2-3 whisper to me." If students respond with different items, have them ask more questions.

➢ Debrief and reflect on the process.

Guess Box
Debrief/Reflect on the Process

It is very important to debrief and reflect on the process after the item is revealed. Ask students the following:

➤ What question helped you (the most) to figure out what was in the box?

➤ Who asked that question? Why did you ask it?

Ask students why they asked specific questions. Discuss with students which questions were important to them and why. What kind of information was gained by these questions?

➤ What are the three most valuable attributes? In other words, if we could only choose three of these words or phrases to describe this object, what would they be?

On the chart paper or SmartBoard, circle or highlight the attributes that the students think are most important in describing the object.

If students disagree, discuss the information that was gained with each attribute and come to consensus.

Share with students why you chose that particular item for the Guess Box. Link back to what they have learned or will learn.

RESOURCE 22

Ideas for Items to Put in a Guess Box

Growth

Item	Suggested Clue(s)
Seed	This is something that you might find outside.
Small plant	Color is an important factor.
An unripe strawberry or tomato	It is edible. (The goal is strawberry and tomato; discuss the fact that they are not ripe after the item is revealed.)
A growth chart	This is something that you hang up. OR This is something that you might find in a doctor's office.

Failure

Item	Suggested Clue(s)
A school paper with an "F" on top	This is something that does not make you happy.
Post-it notes (Invented when another project failed)	This is made of paper.
Chocolate chip cookie (Invented by mistake)	This is something that you can hold in your hand.
Sandpaper (grit)	This is something that has a rough surface.

The Brain

Item	Suggested Clue(s)
Rubber band (neuroplasticity)	This is something that you might find in an office.
Sponge (See *Mindsets in the Classroom* pp. 108–109 for more details)	This is something that you might use when you clean.
Neuron	This is something that is never alone. This is something that can be found inside of your body. (Use this in a guess box after they have been introduced to neurons. It can be used as a group formative assessment to see what they remember about neurons.)

Ready-to-Use Resources for Mindsets in the Classroom © Prufrock Press Inc.

should stay in as a possibility or be removed. If any student can justify why it should stay in, leave it in. You can also bring back any previous categories if a student discovers a common attribute that was not previously mentioned.

As you plan the order of the collection, be sure that the first few items share several common attributes—color, shape, purpose, etc. After many ideas are generated based on these items, create some conceptual conflict by adding an item that does not share many of the same attributes. Be sure to ask for justification for responses that are not obvious. An example of how this might look is included below.

Order of collection:

1. *A checkbook or printout of a checking account from online banking.* Possible responses: things to do with money, things in a purse, things you have to sign, things with numbers. (Students will generate a lot more ideas.)

2. *A cookbook (choose one that has healthy recipes).* What might be eliminated: things to do with money, things you have to sign, things that go in your purse (in some cases a student will bring up the idea that a cookbook could go in your purse so when you are at the grocery store, you can get the ingredients for a recipe). New ideas: Things with pages, things with a cover, things that are rectangular.

3. *A children's book (ballet or ice-skating should be the content).* What might be eliminated: Things in a purse (although some will argue that moms keep their kids' books in their purse, in which case, leave it in). New ideas: Things made of paper, types of books, things that begin with the letter "B."

4. *Three wooden blocks stacked/balanced.* These blocks will cause conceptual conflict for most of the students. What might be eliminated: Books, things made of paper, things in a purse, things with pages, things with a cover, things with numbers. New ideas: Things made from a tree, things that have different parts, things that are becoming obsolete.

5. *An animal on a unicycle toy or a picture of a unicycle.* This will cause conceptual conflict for the rest of the students. What might be eliminated: Things made from a tree, things that start with "B." New ideas: Things for a family, Things that represent different generations.

The last item in this collection is the validator. The validator should help solidify what the common element of the collection is. For this collection, the validator could be any of the following:

⊛ Any toy that requires balance
⊛ A picture of a balance beam
⊛ A balance scale
⊛ A top or bike

It is possible that you have some categories remaining that still work, acknowledge these if you do, then share that the concept that you built the collection around is "balance." Ask students to explain the concept with each item:

- ✹ *Checkbook or printout of a checking account from online banking*—a bank account needs to be balanced (Do not include this item for young students who have no background knowledge about a checkbook.)
- ✹ *Healthy cookbook*—balanced diet
- ✹ *Kids book about ballet or ice-skating*—Ballet and ice-skating require balance; for teachers, the concept could be balanced literacy
- ✹ *Blocks*—They are set up in a way where they are balanced
- ✹ *Unicycle*—Requires balance not to fall off

Ask students for ideas for additional objects that can be added to the collection. Talk about the concept of "balance" and how it can be applied in a variety of ways. For older students, ask for nonexamples—items that would not fit into the collection.

The balance collection can be a vehicle for leading into a math unit that involves balance, balancing equations, or an introduction to algebra. It could also be used to introduce a literary piece that has "balance" as one of its themes.

Resource 23: Collections (pp. 49–50) and Resource 24: Ordering a Serial Collection (pp. 51–52) can help your thinking as you plan for a serial collection.

Critical Reasoning Games

The power of games in learning has been getting more and more popular in the education field. Even though much of the chatter is about digital gaming, a similar outcome can occur with reasoning games that students can hold in their hands. As mentioned above, critical reasoning games became an important part of the Critical Thinking Growth Mindset project and the way they were introduced into the learning process became a critical component. A few guidelines for choosing games to build critical thinking skills:

1. *Identify games for your level of students that are not reading or math skill dependent.* Choose nonverbal games that may build quantitative, analogical, deductive, or inductive reasoning. My favorites include these ThinkFun Games (which can be purchased at http://www.thinkfun.com):
   a. Grades K–1: Swish Jr, Rush Hour Jr, and Robot Turtles
   b. Grades 2–Adult: ShapeOmetry, Chocolate Fix, Brick-by-Brick, Swish, Square-by Square, Gravity Maze, Laser Maze, TipOver, Rush Hour, and Rush Hour Shift

Collections

A collection of objects assembled around a specific concept is used to help students develop classification skills, analyze attributes of objects, and discover relationships between items. It is also a powerful tool for practicing problem-solving skills.

There are two kinds of collections, **serial** and **revealed**. In a revealed collection all objects are displayed at the same time. If the common link between the objects is obvious, a revealed collection works well. Focus would be on finding categories and contrast within the group. A set of toy animals or models of transportation would make an appropriate revealed collection.

A serial collection is used when items are displayed one at a time in a purposeful manner. After each item, the teacher records students' predictions as to what the collection may be focused on. The last item in this collection is the validator. The validator should help solidify what the common element of the collection is.

The order in which the objects are revealed is important. Start with the objects that will generate many possibilities and gradually reveal items with more specificity.

Serial Collection: Things That Were Important to You in the Past

The items are dependent on the student's age—a primary student's collection will look different than a high school student's collection. The sample below could be used with K–2.

1. Bring in the following suggested items in a bag that the students cannot see through or in to:

   ➤ Teddy bear (or Beanie Baby)

   ➤ Scrap of flannel or "blankie"

   ➤ Pacifier

   ➤ A baby board book

   ➤ Birthday card or candle for first birthday

   ➤ Framed picture of a family with a baby/toddler

   ➤ Preschool picture or diploma

   Optional items:

   ➤ Lock of hair

   ➤ Picture or model of a crib, stroller, or playpen

2. Introduce the collection by asking:

   ➤ Do you collect anything?

   ➤ Why do you collect those things?

   ➤ What are some ways that you can add to your collections?

Collections, *continued*

Then tell students: *Today I brought in a collection of things. There is something the same about everything I have in my bag, and I would like for you to try to think of what that may be. I will take the items out one at a time and I'll write down your ideas on these cards (index cards or sticky notes). Let's look at the first item in my collection.*

3. Take the teddy bear or Beanie Baby out. Ask students: *What do you think I may have a collection of?* Record student responses on cards. Possible responses might include bears, stuffed animals, toys, soft things, things that start with "B."

4. Take out the blankie. Tell students: *Let's look at our cards to see if these ideas still work.* Turn cards over if they don't work; have students explain why. Ask: *What other ideas do you have about what this may be a collection of?* Record their responses.

5. Take out the pacifier. Tell students: *Let's look at our cards to see if these ideas still work.* Turn cards over if they don't work; have students explain why. Ask: *What other ideas do you have about what this may be a collection of?* Record their responses. Possible responses might include: things that babies use, soft things, things you sleep with, things that make you happy.

6. Continue with this process until all items in the collection are shown.

7. Acknowledge cards (responses) that are still showing: *All of these ideas you had for my collection work well. Any one of them would work. Good effort and good thinking! Let me tell you what I had in mind when I put this collection together for you. I made this a collection of things that may have been important to you in your past.*

8. Debrief the process with questions like these:

   a. Why would these things be important?

   b. Let's look at this collection. What was important to you in the past? Why? Why are they no longer as important as they once were?

   c. Are any of these things still important to you? Why?

   d. If you could add something to this collection, what would it be?

   e. Why did I put this collection together?

9. Link the collection to an area of study, psychosocial skill, or P21 skill. Possible content connections include:

   a. Social studies—learning about the past

   b. Reading/LA—historical fiction

Ordering a Serial Collection

Concept of collection:

Possible items in my collection:

The first 2–3 items should share many of the same attributes (think about shape, material, purpose, etc.)

A possible order for this collection:

1. _____

Possible student responses:

2. _____

Possible student responses:

3. _____

Possible student responses:

4. _____

Possible student responses:

Ordering a Serial Collection, continued

5. _____

Possible student responses:

6. _____

Possible student responses:

7. _____

Possible student responses:

Which object (do you think) will cause conceptual conflict?

Which object would you select as a validator?

2. *Provide a professional learning opportunity for teachers.* Introduce or review components of neuroplasticity and critical thinking. Introduce each game separately and let the teachers play the games after each introduction for about 10 minutes as partners or individually. Observe behaviors during this time and listen for fixed mindset statements, such as "I am just not a visual-spatial person." Share what you observed and relate it back to growth mindset.

3. *Provide teachers with a timeline and ideas for introducing each game into their classroom.* Some of the games (Rush Hour, Laser Maze, and Chocolate Fix) can be taught by projecting the online version, found at http://www.thinkfun.com/playonline.

4. *Students will keep track of their games with individual game-trackers.* See Resource 25: Game Tracker (pp. 54–55) for an example. Each time they play, they should repeat the last successful level in order to warm up their neural networks.

Students may participate in games during times that the teacher determines. For example, a math teacher may set up ShapeOmetry in his class as an anchor activity that develops quantitative reasoning and perseverance, practices found in the Common Core State Standards for Mathematical Practice. Students can go to the anchor individually or with a partner if they have finished classwork early or if the math teacher is working with another group of students.

Elementary students can access the games during inside recess, as part of small-group math rotation, and as anchor activities.

By allowing students of all levels to build cognitive abilities through these strategies, you allow them to witness their own growth, which is instrumental in building a growth mindset classroom culture.

Game Tracker
I Played These Games!

When you go back to a game, repeat the last level that you did and then move on.

Name: _____

ShapeOmetry		Chocolate Fix		Rush Hour		Brick by Brick		Swish	
Date	Last Level	Date	Last Level	Date	Last Level	Date	Last Level	Date	Last Level

Game Tracker
I Played These Games!

Name: _____

When you go back to a game, repeat the last level that you did and then move on.

Game Name:			Game Name:			Game Name:			Game Name:		
Date	Last Level		Date	Last Level		Date	Last Level		Date	Last Level	

CHAPTER 5

HOW CAN STUDENTS LEARN FROM FAILURE?

Over the past year, I have heard many stories from educators about ways they have transformed their classrooms into environments where students feel safe to make mistakes and fail. These are classrooms where students understand that mistakes are part of the learning process and not a judgment of their intelligence. Students in these classrooms understand that if they are properly challenged, they will struggle and sometimes make mistakes or fail—and that is okay. They use mistakes to reflect on and improve their learning.

"The Gift of Failure: 50 Tips for Teaching Students How to Fail Well" (Chesser, 2013; see http://www.opencolleges.edu.au/informed/features/the-gift-of-failure-50-tips-for-teaching-students-how-to-fail/) provides teachers with tips for how to teach students how to fail. A few of the highlights on the list include:

- ⚙ Teach them to take responsibility.
- ⚙ Teach them to start over. (I would add: Teach them how to evaluate *when* they should start over. Starting over at early stages of struggle does not build grit and resiliency.)
- ⚙ Foster curiosity.
- ⚙ Teach them to innovate.
- ⚙ Let them cry, whine, and complain. (I would add: "Sometimes.")
- ⚙ Teach them to care.
- ⚙ Emphasize humility.

Author Lisa Chesser includes this important note about these 50 tips:

Keep in mind that you may proudly tell yourself that you already do this when you scan over the tips, but there's a pattern and a nuance to teaching students how to fail. These tips connect and complement one another so that the students actually learn and grow from the experience. (para. 7)

Resource 26: Teacher Talking Points on Mistakes and Failure (p. 59) provides a sampling of teacher talking points for mistakes and failure that can be used by teachers with students. These are practices that should be part of everyday learning. Leave this on your desk or tuck it into your planner or gradebook as a reminder of the messaging we need to give students.

Inventions Created by Mistake

Errors and failures can sometimes work out even better then the intended goal—a concept worthy of sharing with your students. *Mistakes That Worked: 40 Familiar Inventions and How They Came To Be* by Charlotte Jones (1994) is a great book for students of all ages. Learning about and discussing one "mistake" a day for 40 days is a great way to infuse dialogue about failure into daily learning. This book highlights how some of the things we eat and use everyday were invented by mistake: the chocolate chip cookie, potato chips, Post-It notes, Slinkys, and penicillin. After discussing the book, students can explore other things that were invented thanks to a failure. Resource 27: Invented by Mistake (p. 60) provides a list of some of the inventions that were created by mistake. These can be also be used for the critical thinking strategy, Feed-BACK (see Chapter 4) or students can research the background of how they came to be. (You can also use Resource 16 in Chapter 4, which includes a list of people who have overcome adversity as a learning experience when discussing failure.)

Failure Quotes

Resource 28: Quotes About Failure (p. 61) provides a list of inspirational quotes about failure. It is not enough just hang these on the walls of the school and classroom. Students need to be given opportunities to interpret and discuss them deeply. Some ideas include:
- ⊛ Students can interpret the quote and see if any differences occur among various student interpretations.

Teacher Talking Points on Mistakes and Failure

➤ Share some of your best, most epic mistakes, then share what you learned from them.

➤ Let students know that failure is their friend—it is an important part of learning.

➤ Use the Think Aloud strategy to demonstrate how you learn from mistakes and failure. (Information about the Think Aloud strategy can be found at https://www.teachervision.com/skill-builder/problem-solving/48546.html)

➤ Discuss the positive aspect of mistakes and failure every day. View errors and failures as "data."

➤ When introducing a new skill or concept:

    ○ Let students know that you welcome mistakes and encourage students to share the errors with everyone so that everyone can learn from them.

    ○ Let students know that you expect that there will be some struggle as they learn new things, which is great because struggle helps make new neural connections and builds resiliency!

➤ Create a safe environment where no one makes fun of or comments on someone else's error in a negative way.

➤ Encourage students to share some their "best" or "epic" errors and what they learned from them.

➤ Keep expectations high and let students know when they have not met those expectations, then tell them what they need to do to improve. Give them the time to re-do the work and offer support in the process.

➤ Circle errors on papers. Let students know that this means, "Look at this again." Provide feedback to them in writing or in person about the errors. (An "X" on a paper teaches nothing.) Allow re-dos.

Invented by Mistake

Post-It© notes

Chocolate chip cookies

Penicillin

Slinky (toy)

Wheaties

Saccharin

Corn flakes

Potato chips

Plastic

Pacemaker

Play-Doh

Champagne

Teflon

Safety glass

Frisbee

Silly putty

Ice cream cone

Super glue

Velcro

Microwave oven

Fireworks

Popsicles

Matches

X-rays

Stainless steel

Quotes About Failure

These quotes can be used in a variety of ways:

- ➤ as part of daily morning announcements,
- ➤ to discuss and interpret with students,
- ➤ to display in classrooms or hallways,
- ➤ to include in parents' weekly bulletin,
- ➤ to learn more about why the person said the quote, and
- ➤ to inspire.

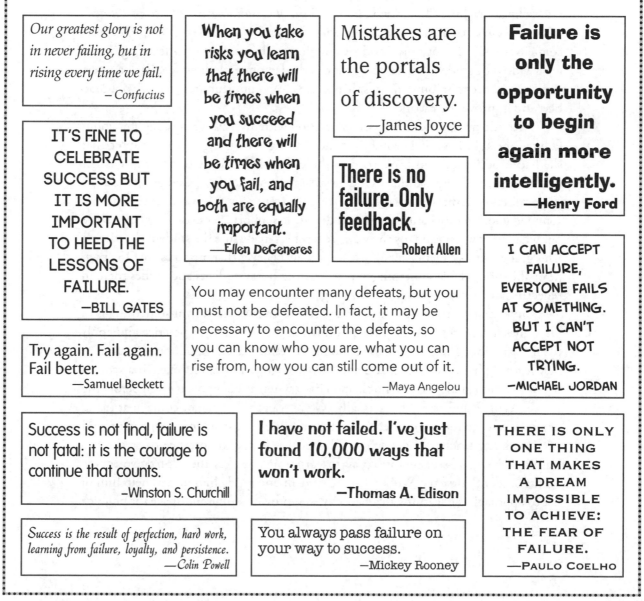

Our greatest glory is not in never failing, but in rising every time we fail.
– Confucius

IT'S FINE TO CELEBRATE SUCCESS BUT IT IS MORE IMPORTANT TO HEED THE LESSONS OF FAILURE.
—BILL GATES

Try again. Fail again. Fail better.
—Samuel Beckett

When you take risks you learn that there will be times when you succeed and there will be times when you fail, and both are equally important.
—Ellen DeGeneres

Mistakes are the portals of discovery.
—James Joyce

There is no failure. Only feedback.
—Robert Allen

You may encounter many defeats, but you must not be defeated. In fact, it may be necessary to encounter the defeats, so you can know who you are, what you can rise from, how you can still come out of it.
—Maya Angelou

Failure is only the opportunity to begin again more intelligently.
—Henry Ford

I CAN ACCEPT FAILURE, EVERYONE FAILS AT SOMETHING. BUT I CAN'T ACCEPT NOT TRYING.
—MICHAEL JORDAN

Success is not final, failure is not fatal: it is the courage to continue that counts.
—Winston S. Churchill

Success is the result of perfection, hard work, learning from failure, loyalty, and persistence.
—Colin Powell

I have not failed. I've just found 10,000 ways that won't work.
—Thomas A. Edison

You always pass failure on your way to success.
—Mickey Rooney

THERE IS ONLY ONE THING THAT MAKES A DREAM IMPOSSIBLE TO ACHIEVE: THE FEAR OF FAILURE.
—PAULO COELHO

⊛ Students can discuss ways that these quotes may or may not resonate with them.

⊛ Students can discuss possible connections to their own life.

⊛ Students can discuss why the quote has endured over time.

⊛ Students can discuss the importance or unimportance of the quote.

Constructive Feedback and Re-Do's

Important to learning from mistakes and failure is knowing how to give and receive constructive, specific feedback without taking it personally and/or having feelings get hurt. The video *Austin's Butterfly: Building Excellence in Student Work—Models, Critique, and Descriptive Feedback* (available at https://vimeo.com/38247060) is not only good viewing for teacher professional learning, but a great video for students in all grades. It clearly demonstrates how feedback and critique can improve an outcome *if* students are given opportunities to work on, practice, and improve their work.

On a side note, I was having a conversation with my 12th-grade daughter about failure. She asked me if I wouldn't mind putting something in this chapter that she had experienced and proceeded to share that many, many teachers in elementary, middle, and high school would always say things to the class like, "It's OK to make mistakes in our class—as long as we learn from them." It was a sentiment that sounded good to me—until she shared that little support ever existed to help figure out what went wrong and, by the way, the teachers made sure the students knew that "This grade counts." Her point? If a teacher truly believes that mistakes are OK, then he or she should have something in place that supports students and guides them in reflecting and analyzing what went wrong.

Allow them to re-do assignments and retake assessments only if something is in place that will help them learn the information in a new way or practice and apply the information. There is no sense in doing something over again if no reflection or new learning has taken place. A math teacher might allow a test retake if a score is below a certain grade—this is not helpful if no systematic support is given before the retake. As my daughter said, it's usually, "Go over in that corner or come in at recess or after school to retake your test"—with no additional instruction, support, or guidance from the teacher. If a teacher truly believes in the importance of errors as a learning device and students are trying to learn from mistakes, then don't give a grade on the student's first try. Work with the student and guide him or her, help him or her to approach the learning in a new way, and provide a time and space for practice.

Find Texts With Authentic Stories of Failure

The National Geographic website has a great article for students in grades 7–12 that looks at famous explorers and how failure plays a part in exploration called "Famous Failures: Failure Is an Option" by Hannah Bloch (see http://ngm.nationalgeographic.com/2013/09/famous-failures/bloch-text; this is also a nice piece of text to read in conjunction with the novel, *Shackleton's Stowaway*). Lots of discussion points are evident in this article, for example:

"I learned how *not* to climb the first four times I tried to summit Everest," says alpinist Pete Athans, who's reached the world's highest peak seven times. "Failure gives you a chance to refine your approach. You're taking risks more and more intelligently." (para. 4)

Identify texts that give real accounts of the value of failure so that students can see how failure can have a positive impact in many aspects of life.

Video Resources

The final failure resource, Resource 29: Failure Videos (p. 64), is a list of videos that can supplement your class discussions around failure. Use these to fuel interest and to stimulate discussion surrounding mistakes and failure. All of these resources contribute toward a risk-free environment for optimal student learning.

Failure Videos

Video Title	Address	Summary	Grade Level	Length
Famous Failures	https://www.youtube.com/watch?v=zlYEClijmnQs	Features failures faced by Michael Jordan Albert Einstein, Oprah Winfrey, Walt Disney, Lionel Messi, Steve Jobs, Eminem, Thomas Edison, The Beatles, Dr. Seuss, and Abraham Lincoln.	6–12	3 minutes
Michael Jordan Failure Commercial	https://www.youtube.com/watch?v=45mMioJ5szc	As Jordan says in this Nike commercial: "I've missed more than 9,000 shots in my career. I've lost almost 300 games. Twenty-six times I've been trusted to take the game winning shot . . . and missed. I've failed over and over and over again in my life. And that is why I succeed."	K–12	30 seconds
Meet the Robinsons Failure Scene	https://www.youtube.com/watch?v=TNXr5Alytg4	When Lewis tries to fix a gadget but fails, he feels down on himself, but the rest of the Robinson family cheer and celebrate his failure.	K–8	1 minute
Courage of Famous Failures—Inspirational	https://www.youtube.com/watch?v=YdeyI0vXdP0	This video talks about legendary public figures who didn't give up after failing.	5–12	4.5 minutes
25 Accidental Inventions That Changed The World	https://www.youtube.com/watch?v=pf_Qv3q0M_c	This video features 25 inventions that no one actually intended to invent—we have them due to mistakes and failure.	K–12	9 minutes
Embracing Kids' Failure	https://www.youtube.com/watch?v=Bj3xetxg6fY	This video for parents is part of a discussion series put on by the Greater Good Science Center about embracing children's failures so that they learn to take on challenges.	Parents	4 minutes

Ready-to-Use Resources for Mindsets in the Classroom © Prufrock Press Inc.

CHAPTER 6

WHAT MESSAGES SHOULD PARENTS HEAR ABOUT GROWTH MINDSETS?

Here they are, the most requested resources that I have received since the release of *Mindsets in the Classroom*. In *Mindsets in the Classroom*, readers are provided with sample newsletter blurbs (these can be found later on in this chapter), but educators want more. They want parents to use the same language and be on the same page as district and school staff. Educators want parents to understand that mistakes and failure are part of the learning process and struggle is not a bad thing. Schools have tried myriad experiences to get parents involved: book clubs, growth mindset game nights, principal coffees, and professional learning workshops for parents. If possible, have parents involved with planning your growth mindset school community. Invite a few parent representatives to be part of a school or district Mindset Committee or invite them to a Leadership Team meeting when plans are being made. Being part of the planning and encouraging parent input not only helps them understand the content more deeply, but also allows parents some ownership of the process and forms a partnership with a common goal. In turn, they will talk to other parents at the bus stop, at the sports field, at church, and at neighborhood gatherings.

This chapter provides some resources that will help educators reach out and communicate with the greater parent community. Schools with diverse student populations must keep in mind that these resources should be translated into other languages and parent meetings/workshops must be made accessible to the majority of your parent community. Plan a Growth Mindset Parent Night, making it as accessible as possible for your community to attend. Consider providing free babysitting (high school students who need community service hours work well) and/or provide pizza or dessert/coffee. Create a welcoming environment so that it will attract a great number of parents/guardians.

Introduce Growth Mindset Step-by-Step

After a Growth Mindset Parent Night, or a brief introduction to fixed and growth mindsets on Back-to-School Night or before a PTA meeting, Resource 30: Ideas for Creating a Growth Mindset Environment at Home (pp. 67–70) can be used. This resource is broken down in to seven sections, each focusing on a different goal toward helping parents develop a growth mindset home environment. Schools should send each part out separately so that parents can focus on changes a little at a time. If too much information is given at once, it decreases the chance that it will be read in its entirety. (I'll admit: I am quite guilty of just skimming extended notices that my kids bring home or are sent out electronically.)

Breaking it down into small steps will also increase the chance that families will participate because it becomes more doable and not so overwhelming. This is particularly helpful for families whose practice is more "fixed" than "growth." These steps can be sent home (on paper or electronically) weekly, every few weeks, or monthly. It would also be interesting to create an online space (blog or Facebook group) where parents can share their ideas, struggles, and questions as they embrace a growth mindset philosophy. Schools and districts can also add more specific ideas related to their community, such as a local rock-climbing wall or library reading program that might require perseverance from the children.

Set Up a Growth Mindset Parent Webpage

Your school or district may also want to set up a Growth Mindset Parent Webpage. This can be updated as new resources become available. Resource 31: Sample Parent Webpage Screenshot (p. 71) is a sample of a webpage that would be helpful for parents and guardians. Schools and districts can also access this website by visiting http://www.prufrock.com/assets/clientpages/mindset_webpage.aspx.

Not interested in building a webpage? You may want to include some of the web links in Resource 32: Growth Mindset Links (p. 72) in your school or classroom bulletin.

Ideas for Creating a Growth Mindset Environment at Home

Ideas for Creating a Growth Mindset Environment at Home Part 1:
Parents Work Toward a Growth Mindset for Themselves

➤ We can't expect our children to have a growth mindset if we don't have one ourselves. Recognize fixed mindset thinking in yourself and talk yourself into a growth mindset. This can also be done out loud so that your child can hear how you are changing your mindset. For example, you might catch yourself saying, "I can't figure out how to fill out this document." Then quickly rephrase it to add, "I think I need to check on the website or call the bank so I can ask some questions. Then I am sure I will be able to fill it out accurately."

➤ Be aware of your own fixed mindset statements such as "I am a terrible cook," "I was never good at math either," or "I wish I could play the piano like you do." (You can, with practice and perseverance!)

➤ Be aware of blaming genetics for anything—both positive and negative.

➤ Be careful about comparing your kids to their siblings or other kids.

➤ We want our children to enjoy the process of learning—not just be successful. Model this concept at home. For example, after a less than desirable outcome trying to bake something challenging, you might say "I really learned a lot making those cookies" rather than "Ugghh, what a waste of time. That was an epic fail. I will never try that recipe again."

Ideas for Creating a Growth Mindset Environment at Home Part 2:
Using Growth Mindset Praise and Feedback

➤ Praise what your child does, not who he or she is. Instead of saying, "You are so smart/clever/brilliant," say "I can see you really worked hard/put forth effort/tried hard." Praise perseverance and resiliency when you see your child struggle or face challenge. Avoid praising grades. Focus on praising work ethic and effort—not achievement.

➤ Adopt the word "yet" into your vocabulary. If your child proclaims that he doesn't understand something, can't dribble a basketball, or can't play a song on his guitar, remind him that he can't "yet" but with hard work he will have success.

➤ Avoid comparing your child's success with that of siblings or friends—achievement is not a competition. There is enough success for everyone.

Ideas for Creating a Growth Mindset Environment at Home Part 3:
Redirecting Fixed Mindset Thinking

➤ Redirect your child's fixed mindset statements. If you hear your child say "I am no good in math" or "I just can't understand Shakespeare," point out the fixed mindset thinking and direct her to a growth mindset place. Remind her that she may not understand yet, but will by asking questions, finding new strategies, setting small goals, and working hard. Two examples of how to redirect such statements are included below.

If Your Child Says	Then You Might Say
"I am no good in math."	"You may not understand this yet, so let's practice some more."
"I don't need to study; I always do well on math assessments."	"Studying can help prime the brain for further growth. Maybe you should let your teacher know that these assessments don't require much practice for you and that you are willing to take on more challenge."

Ideas for Creating a Growth Mindset Environment at Home Part 4:
Struggle

➤ Help your child become curious about errors or lack of success. Remind your child that failure is important on the way to success. Model this!

➤ Show your child the Michael Jordan *Failure* commercial (available at https://www.youtube.com/watch?v=45mMioJ5szc and only 30 seconds long). Talk to your child about what the last line of the video means.

➤ Provide some puzzles and games that may create a little struggle for your child. Work together and discuss why struggle shows that you are learning and that you can build resiliency.

➤ Model and encourage resiliency—the ability to bounce back from errors and failures.

Ideas for Creating a Growth Mindset Environment at Home Part 5:
Flexibility and Optimism

➤ Model flexibility. Communicate that change is an important part of living life. Model this by taking a flexible mentality when things don't go as planned. Don't let frustrating situations get the best of you—make your children aware of your ability to adapt due to a change in plans. Praise your children for their flexibility and adaptability when plans change or success is not met.

➤ Model optimism. Adopt a "glass half full" mentality in your home. A person with "hope" believes there can be a positive side to most situations.

➤ Play a game with your kids: For every time something happens that is perceived as "bad," try to find the good in every situation. This game can get a little silly but it gets a message of positivity across. For example, when a glass is accidentally broken, a possible response might be, "Now we have more room on our shelf!"

Ideas for Creating a Growth Mindset Environment at Home Part 6:
Learning and the Brain

➤ Talk about neural networking. Ask your child what he or she has learned in school about the brain.

➤ Whenever you hear your child say "I give up" or "I just don't get this," remind your child to visualize neurons connecting every time he learns something new. Encourage your child to work hard and practice new skills and concepts so that he can develop strong neural connections in his brain.

➤ Share with your child some things that you have not yet mastered and your plan for practicing and building stronger connections in your brain.

Ideas for Creating a Growth Mindset Environment at Home Part 7:
Developing Important Psychosocial Skills

➢ A child's innate ability contributes to only about 25% of achievement. The other 75% are psychosocial skills that must be deliberately developed.

The important skills we can help our children develop include:

- perseverance,
- self-confidence,
- resiliency,
- coping skills for disappointment and failure, and
- the ability to handle constructive feedback.

➢ Choose books to read with younger students that highlight characters that demonstrate these skills. Discuss these with your child.

➢ When watching TV or a movie with your kids, talk about a character's strength or lack of perseverance or resiliency. Ask your children how the situation or story would be different if the person did or did not have this skill.

➢ Name the psychosocial skills words and use phrases that represent these around the house. For example, you might say, "My supervisor gave me some constructive feedback about how I can do my job better. I am grateful for that because she gave me some new things to try" or "I was watching you (climb that tree, play that video game, figure out the new cell phone, etc.) today. You really showed determination and perseverance!"

Sample Parent Webpage Screenshot

Prufrock Press

Gifted Education • Advanced Learning
Twice-Exceptional Learners • Special Needs Students

Prufrock Search

Search

Browse Catalog

NEW FOR SPRING 2015

Best Sellers

Advanced Curriculum ▸

College Planning

Common Core Standards

Creative Kids Magazine

Differentiation Resources

Gifted Child Education ▸

Language Arts ▸

Leadership and Social Skills

Math ▸

Philosophy

Parenting Gifted Children

Science ▸

Social Studies ▸

Special Needs ▸

Teaching and Planning Ideas

Technology

Thinking Skills ▸

All Titles ▸

Sample Parent Webpage

Building a Growth Mindset Culture at Home

Our school/district is committed to developing a growth mindset school environment—a place where all students believe that with effort and perseverance, they can succeed. Dr. Carol Dweck, a researcher at Stanford University, has identified two belief systems about intelligence.

More About Fixed and Growth Mindset

A *fixed* **mindset** is one where we believe that our children's innate abilities, talents, and intelligence are fixed. They are either "good" or talented at something or they are not. They can certainly learn new things, but this particular skill or subject is not really their "thing."

How many of you have ever thought to yourself (or said out loud), "My daughter probably isn't very good in math because I was not very good in math." Or, "I was not good in high school English, so I guess my son takes after me." These are examples of fixed mindset thinking. Even a perceived positive statement like, "He has a God-given talent in_____" or " He is a born leader" demonstrates fixed mindset thinking.

As a parent, you may have fixed mindset thinking about your own abilities; you may think, " I can't cook", "I can't dance; I have two left feet", "I leave that to my wife/husband, I can't figure it out."

A *growth mindset* is the belief that intelligence, skills, and talent are malleable, and they can change with effort, perseverance, and practice. Neuroscience explains this as neuroplasticity. We can all get "smarter."

This 4-minute video, Fostering Growth Mindsets is part of a discussion series created by the Greater Good Science center between Christine Carter (sociologist, mom, and "happiness expert") and Kelly Corrigan (author and mom) about how moving toward a growth-oriented mindset can give your children the drive to succeed.

So, we never want to say things like this to our children:

- Some people are just not science (or fill in the subject of choice) people.
- Writing (or art, math, etc.) comes naturally for you.
- Look at that, you did that without even trying.
- You have a God-given talent.

These are all fixed mindset statements. We need to focus feedback on what a child does, not who he or she is. We never, ever want to say things like, "You are so smart!" Click on the links below to find out why:

- How to Praise Children
- Carol Dweck: A Study on Praise and Mindsets

One of the most frequently used words in your vocabulary should be the word *yet*, such as, " You are not quite getting it yet, but with practice, you will." A couple of links to help you use this word more often are:

- Carol Dweck: The Power of Yet
- Sesame Street: Janelle Monae: Power of Yet

Learning From Failure

From the moment our children are born, we want to protect them. Our instincts are to catch them before they fall. It is not easy seeing our children not have success in whatever goal they are working toward—from learning to walk to getting into their first choice of college. But in order to raise resilient, confident, optimistic children, we must learn to be comfortable when they make mistakes and/or fail. When children are given opportunities to struggle, it builds resiliency. Without struggle it is difficult to develop coping skills, grit, and resiliency. As parents, we must model this as well; let your kids see you being persistent and overcoming challenges—not quitting because something is "too hard."

http://www.prufrock.com/assets/clientpages/mindset_webpage.aspx

Growth Mindset Links

The following links can be included in school, district, or classroom bulletins.

Moving Toward Growth Mindset

The following link will help with your goals in moving toward a growth mindset:

➤ Fostering Growth Mindsets (https://www.youtube.com/watch?v=vsP43BqinQY): This 4-minute video, *Fostering Growth Mindsets*, is part of a discussion series created by the Greater Good Science Center between Christine Carter (sociologist, mom, and happiness expert) and Kelly Corrigan (author and mom) about moving toward a growth-oriented mindset.

Growth Mindset Praise

The following links are centered on growth mindset praise:

➤ How to Praise Children (https://www.youtube.com/watch?v=4vUAxlLi0Zo): This is another part of a discussion series created by the Greater Good Science Center between Christine Carter and Kelly Corrigan about how praising your children can make them feel great and strive to be even greater.

➤ Carol Dweck—A Study on Praise and Mindsets (https://www.youtube.com/watch?v=NWv1VdDeoRY): This is a great synthesis of Carol Dweck's research about the effects that praise has on our children. CEO and cofounder of the Championship Basketball School, Trevor Ragan, presents the data highlighting the differences in praising intelligence versus praising effort.

The Importance of "Yet"

The following are links about the importance of the word "yet":

➤ Carol Dweck on the Power of Yet (https://www.youtube.com/watch?v=ZyAde4nIIm8): This video contains a summary of the importance of the word "yet" in about 1 minute.

➤ Sesame Street: Janelle Monae—Power of Yet (https://www.youtube.com/watch?v=XLeUvZvuvAs): This is an engaging video with the Sesame Street friends learning about the power of "yet" through a song sung by R&B singer Janelle Monae.

Learning From Failure

To read more about learning from failure, consider these links:

➤ The Importance of Mistakes: Helping Children Learn From Failure (http://www.brighthorizons.com/family-resources/e-family-news/2013-the-importance-of-mistakes-helping-children-learn-from-failure/): This article provides ideas for parents for encouraging risk-taking and helping them learn from their errors.

➤ Allow Your Children to Learn From Failure (http://www.thenownews.com/community/allow-your-children-to-learn-from-failure-1.1386910): Parenting columnist Kathy Lynn explains why failure is not a bad experience for our children in this video.

➤ How Children Learn From Failure (http://www.enannysource.com/blog/index.php/2014/01/22/how-children-learn-from-failure/): This article, written for both parents and childcare providers, provides a list of strategies to try when your child is facing failure.

Have Students Spread the Word

Another great resource for communicating with parents are students themselves! As students learn more and more about the malleability of their mind and the importance of a growth mindset, ask them to share the information with their parents, perhaps starting with a letter like the one below.

> Hi Mom/Dad,
> We are learning about growth mindset in school. Did you know that our brains are like muscles and the more we exercise them, the smarter we get? I would like to talk to you about some of the things that I have learned about having a growth mindset.
> Love,
> Your Son/Daughter

Students may also be assigned an open-ended assignment where they are asked to come up with a way to share what they know about growth mindset with their family—emphasize doing this creatively, not just a discussion around the dinner table or a conversation when driving to a practice. Some elementary and middle schools have held Growth Mindset Family Game Nights. Parents and students were invited to participate in an evening that began with information about mindsets and why a growth mindset is important. Then, parents partnered with their child to play some reasoning games. (I like many of the reasoning games from ThinkFun such as ShapeOmetry, Chocolate Fix, Brick-by-Brick, and Rush Hour. These games, and many more, can be found at http://www.thinkfun.com.)

The students had played the games previously and taught their parents how to play. This was fun for the students, but many of the parents began to struggle as the levels became more difficult. Teacher-leaders of the game night pointed out to parents that struggle creates neural connections in the brain and that the more they play, the stronger those connections become. They encouraged them to not give up and persevere—they modeled the growth mindset language that parents could use with their own children. The schools followed up with newsletter reminders like the ones found on Resource 33: Parent Newsletter Blurbs (pp. 74–76).

Parent Newsletter Blurbs

Parent Newsletter Blurbs in English

First Newsletter Installment

One way that parents can really help their children is by carefully choosing the words that are used when they praise them. Every word parents say and action they perform sends a message to their children. These words and actions tell children how to think about themselves. Parents should always praise their child's effort instead of praising accomplishments. The following table includes some examples.

Do Not Say	Do Say
You are really athletic!	You really work hard and pay attention when you are on that field!
You are so smart!	You work hard in school and it shows!
Your drawing is wonderful; you are my little artist.	I can see you have been practicing your drawing; what a great improvement!
You are a great athlete. You could be the next Pelé!	Keep practicing, and you will see great results!
You always get good grades; that makes me happy.	When you put forth effort, it really shows in your grades. You should be so proud of yourself. We are proud of you!

So the next time you are ready to praise your child, stop and think about how to use that opportunity to praise his or her effort instead of accomplishments.

Second Newsletter Installment

In the last installment of [*name of school newsletter*], parents were given suggestions about ways to praise their children. Research suggests that parents should think twice about praising our kids for being "smart" or "talented," because this may foster a *fixed mindset*. Instead, if we encourage our kids' efforts and acknowledge their persistence and hard work, then we will support their development of a *growth mindset*. Children with a growth mindset believe that with effort and persistence they can learn and achieve in school. A growth mindset will better equip them to persevere and pick themselves up when things do not go their way. Parents should also examine their own belief systems. Do you have a growth mindset? Do you believe that with effort, persistence, and motivation your children can achieve their goals?

Dr. Carol Dweck, an educational researcher states,

Parents should not shield their children from challenges, mistakes, and struggles. Instead, parents should teach children to love challenges. They can say things like "This is hard. What fun!" or "This is too easy. It's no fun." They should teach their children to embrace mistakes, "Oooh, here's an interesting mistake. What should we do next?" And they should teach them to love effort: "That was a fantastic struggle. You really stuck to it and made great progress" or "This will take a lot of effort—boy, will it be fun."

Some parents need to work at having a growth mindset. It takes time and practice, but it is well worth it when you see the difference that it makes in your children!

Parent Newsletter Blurbs in Spanish

First Newsletter Installment

Una forma en que los padres pueden realmente ayudar a sus hijos es escogiendo cuidadosamente las palabras que usan para elogiarlos. Todas las palabras que los padres utilizan y sus acciones transmiten un mensaje a sus hijos. Dichas palabras y acciones manifiestan a sus hijos cómo pensar acerca de sí mismos. Los padres siempre deben elogiar el esfuerzo de sus hijos, en vez de elogiar solamente sus logros. Por ejemplo:

No Diga	Diga
¡Eres un verdadero deportista!	¡Realmente te esmeras mucho y prestas atención cuando estás en el campo de juego!
¡Eres tan inteligente!	¡Trabajas mucho en la escuela y se nota!
Tu dibujo es maravilloso; tú eres mi pequeño artista.	Se nota que has estado practicando dibujar; ¡cómo has mejorado!
Eres un gran deportista. ¡Tú podrías ser el próximo Pelé! (o usando el nombre de otro deportista)	¡Continúa practicando y verás grandes resultados!
Tú siempre tienes buenas calificaciones; eso me alegra mucho.	Cuando te esfuerzas, realmente se nota en tus calificaciones. Deberías sentirte muy orgulloso/a de ti mismo/a. ¡Estamos orgullosos de ti!

Así que la próxima vez que usted vaya a elogiar a su hijo/a, deténgase y piense cómo usar esa oportunidad para elogiar su esfuerzo y no sus logros.

Second Newsletter Installment

En el último fascículo de [*nombre del boletín de noticas de la escuela*], se ofrecieron sugerencias a los padres sobre cómo elogiar a sus hijos. Las investigaciones sugieren que los padres deberían pensar dos veces antes de elogiar a sus hijos por ser "inteligentes" o "talentosos", ya que esto puede fomentar una *actitud fija*. En cambio, si estimulamos el esfuerzo en nuestros hijos, si damos reconocimiento a la perseverancia y al trabajo fuerte, apoyaremos su evolución hacia una *actitud de crecimiento*. Los niños que poseen una actitud de crecimiento pasan a creer que con esfuerzo y perseverancia aprenderán y podrán desempeñarse bien en sus estudios. Una actitud de crecimiento los equipará mejor para tener perseverancia y para levantar el ánimo cuando las cosas no son como ellos desearían. Los padres deberían también examinar sus propias formas de pensar. ¿Posee usted una actitud de crecimiento? ¿Cree usted que con esfuerzo, perseverancia y motivación sus hijos pueden alcanzar sus metas? La Dra. Carol Dweck, investigadora educacional, manifiesta,

Los padres no deben proteger a sus hijos de los desafíos, errores y luchas. En su lugar, los padres deberían enseñar a sus hijos a amar el desafío. Ellos pueden decir cosas como "Esto es difícil. ¡Qué divertido!" o "Esto es demasiado fácil. No es divertido." Ellos deben enseñar a sus hijos a aceptar los errores, "Ah, aquí hay un error interesante. ¿Qué deberíamos hacer ahora?" Y ellos deberían enseñarles a amar el esfuerzo: "Esa fue una lucha fantástica. Realmente te mantuviste en pie y lograste un gran progreso." O, "Esto va a tomar mucho esfuerzo—pero mira que será divertido."

Algunos padres necesitan trabajar para lograr tener una Actitud de Crecimiento. ¡Eso toma tiempo y práctica, pero realmente vale la pena cuando se nota la diferencia que hace en sus hijos!

Note. From *Mindsets in the Classroom* (pp. 163–167) by M. C. Ricci, 2013, Waco, TX: Prufrock Press. Copyright 2013 by Prufrock Press. Reprinted with permission.

Make Growth Mindset Front and Center

When parents enter your school building, can they tell it is a place that celebrates growth? A bulletin board that celebrates progress greets you when you enter Kemptown Elementary School in Frederick County, MD. Principal Kristen Canning is committed to celebrating growth in her building. You can see photos of her bulletin board in Resource 34: Sample Growth Mindset Bulletin Board (p. 77). Teachers may want to create their own boards in classrooms or shared spaces.

Her message to parents:

> We will be celebrating progress on our growth mindset bulletin board in the front lobby, posting examples of students who have made impressive gains toward their target. It's important that students' efforts are recognized and that we celebrate growth—it is what motivates people to keep working!

The partnership between school and home is imperative when helping students develop and maintain a growth mindset. The resources provided can be tweaked to suit your specific school, classroom, or district needs. Just keep the reminders going all year long so that parents realize this is something that will stay—not a passing fad.

Sample Growth Mindset Bulletin Board

CHAPTER 7

CAN GIFTED EDUCATION AND A GROWTH MINDSET BELIEF COEXIST?

The tide is turning in the world of gifted education. Educators and parents are realizing that is not the label of *gifted* that is important (in fact, that label may perpetuate fixed mindset thinking). What is important is developing growth mindset thinking and addressing unmet needs for all students. At the 2014 annual convention of the National Association for Gifted Children in Baltimore, MD, a panel of researchers was convened to share their thoughts on the future of gifted education. One statement really stood out for me. James Borland, Professor of Education at Columbia Teachers College, shared this observation about the identification of gifted students, "It is time we stop asking if he or she is gifted and instead ask, what are his or her needs?"

Since the release of *Mindsets in the Classroom*, I have discovered a new favorite book, *Beyond Gifted Education: Designing and Implementing Advanced Academic Programs* (Peters, Matthews, McBee, & McCoach, 2013). *Beyond Gifted Education* challenges us to get away from the need to label our children and instead spend time determining what their individual, instructional needs are. The traditional structure in American education does not always meet the needs of all students, particularly our high-potential and advanced learners. We are required to think of innovative ways and brainstorm possibilities for students who need a different learning experience. We cannot let the confines of a school schedule, a child's age, or whether they have met an arbitrary cut-off score (all of which represent fixed mindset) for "gifted and talented" put a ceiling on a student's possibilities.

Beyond Gifted Education (2013) shared the authors' Advanced Academic model. This model includes identifying unmet academic needs, making sure there are services available, and finding students who would benefit from a specific advanced academic service, regardless of how a child is labeled or the classes in which he or she is placed. The inspiration for Resource 35: Guidance Document for Advanced

Learning Opportunities: Determining and Planning for Students' Unmet Advanced Academic Needs (pp. 81–82) is the Advanced Academic model described in *Beyond Gifted Education*. This resource is just one possible way to discuss and determine ways to meet high-potential students' unmet academic needs. I encourage you to customize this guidance document for your own school/district. This should be completed with several educators around the table: classroom teacher(s), administrator, "GT" teacher (if you have one), and perhaps a content area department head at the secondary level.

The intention of this resource is to begin a discussion about students who have unmet needs. If no service, curriculum, or instructional experience exists in your school to meet the students' needs, then the team needs to brainstorm possibilities that may not have previously existed or been offered to students. For example, a middle school student could go to the local high school for an Algebra 2 class or three grade 4 students could be brought together from their various classrooms to form an intellectual peer group and various teachers could work together to meet their advanced academic needs. High school students might be set up with an online course, be able to take a class at a local community college, or conduct an independent research project with a community mentor. Perhaps you are a large district who has academically advanced outliers in neighborhood schools—when a child has no intellectual peer group, I have seen instances where parents pull them out to homeschool—instead of losing these high-potential learners, why not form an Advanced Learning Center and pull those kids together in one place?

Dr. Scott J. Peters, Associate Professor of Educational Foundations at the University of Wisconsin-Whitewater, is one of the authors of *Beyond Gifted Education*. Dr. Peters also wrote a piece for *Creativity Post*, "The Bright vs. Gifted Comparison: A Distraction From What Matters" (published July 10, 2014). This piece can serve as a wonderful vehicle for reflection and discussion during a professional development workshop for administrators and/or teachers. It is adapted with a few updates from Dr. Peters in Resource 36: Professional Development Resource: Bright vs. Gifted (pp. 83–86).

Dr. Peters's article also speaks to one of the important components of a growth mindset environment (as mentioned in Chapter 1): Equitable Access to Advanced Learning Opportunities. Whether a child is "bright" or "gifted" should not matter—any child should be given access to challenge if he or she has the capability, potential, or motivation to take it on. Using articles like this with staff really helps people dig down deep into their belief systems and reflect upon their own mindsets in an authentic way.

Guidance Document for Advanced Learning Opportunities: Determining and Planning for Students' Unmet Advanced Academic Needs

Student:_____ Date: _____

Grade/Content Area:_____

Engagement in Learning

Students who are not sufficiently challenged may be disengaged in learning due to lack of rigor or perceived value of work. Circle the student's engagement using the scale below.

1	2	3	4	5
Disengaged Uninterested– sees no value in tasks.		**Somewhat Engaged** Completes work but sees little value in the experience.		**Highly Engaged** Sees value in learning experiences.

Evidence of Potential Unmet Need(s)

Consider current level of mastery, review standard and advanced curriculum through the lens of student need(s), and consider differentiation that has already occurred for the student. Discuss the following data:

Preassessment/Diagnostic Data:_____

Formative Assessment Data: _____

Summative/Achievement Data Review: _____

Anecdotal Data: _____

Other Data: _____

Parent Input

_____

_____

_____

_____

_____

Observation of Noncognitive Factors (Perseverance/Resiliency/Motivation/Work Ethic)

_____

_____

_____

_____

What Instructional Options Are Available to Help Address Any Unmet Needs?

Possibilities:

➤ Exposure to advanced academics (with support/scaffolding as needed)
➤ Instruction of above grade level standards within regular class
➤ On-level standards with deep enrichment/critical thinking opportunities within regular classroom
➤ Participation in Honors or above-level course(s)
➤ Cross-class cluster grouping to form intellectual peer group
➤ Cross-grade grouping to meet content area strength
➤ Blended or personalized learning opportunity through technology
➤ Elementary student attending middle school for an advanced class
➤ Middle school student attending high school for an advanced class
➤ High school student taking an online college course or attending a local college for an advanced course

Other Services/Programming That Could Occur

_____

_____

_____

What (if Any) Professional Learning Should Occur to Support Teachers With Meeting These Student Needs?

_____

_____

_____

Professional Learning Resource: Bright vs. Gifted

As you read the following piece, highlight areas that: make you pause and think, you agree or disagree with, or give you an "a-ha" moment. We will discuss after the reading.

The Bright vs. Gifted Comparison: A Distraction From What Matters
Scott J. Peters, Ph.D.

Anyone who is in the field of gifted and talented education has probably come across the "bright vs. gifted" or "bright child vs. gifted learner" form. It appears to have first shown up in a 1989 article in *Challenge Magazine* by Janice Szabos but was likely around in alternate forms long before that. You can find a few links to it at the end of this article—it's not hard to find and seems to be one of the most ubiquitous publications related to gifted education. I have seen this form included in formal district gifted education plans and even posted to state department of education websites. The overall suggestion seems to be that as a teacher, educationally useful information comes from knowing if one of your students is "just bright" vs. if she is "truly" gifted. In other words, if two children are otherwise identical in their level of achievement, aptitude, creativity, etc., they should still be treated differently if one is "truly" gifted and one is "just" bright.

The distinction of whether a child is bright vs. gifted is really emblematic of many of the challenges facing the field of gifted education. Let's imagine for a moment that two identical children walk into your classroom (you playing the role of teacher). Both are very interested in the topic and have already mastered what you were going to teach over the next several weeks. Both ask good, probing questions and draw connections to other topics. Both prefer working with others who are at their academic level and can handle some degree of independent work. You now have two options.

Option #1: You provide them both with a more challenging course of study in-line with the students' skill area and then check in frequently to make sure they both remain challenged and engaged.

Option #2: You go home and spend some time trying to decide if one of the kids is gifted whereas the other is just bright.

Now the million dollar question: what is gained by first diagnosing giftedness as opposed to moving straight to the providing of more challenging material? What about the distinction of "bright vs. gifted" is educationally helpful *if the students are otherwise the same in what they need from their school or teacher?*

The "bright vs. gifted" form, while a seemingly easy way to communicate the population of interest in gifted education, also serves to take up time from already-busy educators that could better be focused on developing interventions and providing services. A secondary issue is that many of the characteristics presented of a "gifted" learner are more likely to be observed in students from dominant cultural groups (Peterson, 1999). A tertiary issue is that identifying some students as bright and some as gifted as a trait of their person (as opposed to a temporary state) further reinforces an entity view of ability and the self (Dweck, 2007; Ricci, 2013).

Bright or gifted? Who cares? Either way, schools need to make sure both students are being appropriately challenged. Over the last few years I have become increasingly concerned that many gifted education programs and professionals don't seem to see "bright kids" as part of their purview. I've seen students performing seven or eight grade levels above their age peers who are turned away from gifted services because their IQs aren't above 130 or because they seemed to fall more in the "bright" category than the "gifted" category on the aforementioned form. They are drastically under challenged in school but because they are not considered gifted they are ignored by the very system that should be their champion.

Many people will likely respond to this position with points about the unique social and emotional needs of gifted students—needs that apparently don't exist for "bright" students. Jim Delisle argued recently that knowing a child is gifted and providing him that label assures access to services. Besides the fact that this statement is blatantly false (for example, Wisconsin legally mandates gifted identification and services in grades K–12 and yet very few schools actually do so), why can't we proceed directly from Step 1: recognizing the child is unchallenged, to Step 3: providing an intervention that will result in appropriate challenge? What is gained by adding an intervening step regarding the diagnosis of giftedness or the distinction of bright vs. gifted? See Figure 1 from Peters, McBee, Matthews, & McCoach (2014). Why do we need to go through Step 2 or checking to first make sure the child is really gifted and not just bright?

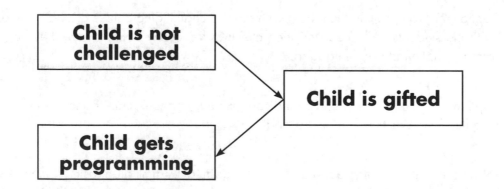

Let me be abundantly clear about something. I do believe gifted individuals exist.

That is to say that I believe there are people who experience the world in qualitatively different ways and take in greater stimulation from a given amount of environmental stimuli than is typical in a given population. My concern is that focusing on this population *in the context of K–12 gifted education* really misses the boat when it comes to the purposes of such programs (and the purposes of public education). Some (not all) "gifted" children are under challenged in their learning in schools. Likewise, some under challenged children are also gifted. But these two groups are not *inherently* the same population of people. Why can't the field just focus on looking for those who are unchallenged, and have as a goal assuring they become challenged and remain so as much of the time as possible, instead of spending so much time on first diagnosing giftedness?

Links to the Bright vs. Gifted Comparison

➢ http://www.bownet.org/besgifted/brightvs.htm

➢ http://www.ode.state.or.us/teachlearn/specialty/tag/r5brightchild.pdf

References

Dweck, C. (2007). *Mindset: The new psychology of success.* New York: Ballantine Books.

McBee, M. T., McCoach, D. B., Peters, S. J., & Matthews, M. S. (2012). The case for a schism: Commentary on Subotnik, Olszewki-Kubilius, and Worrell (2011). *Gifted Child Quarterly, 56,* 210–214.

Peters, S. J., Matthews, M., McCoach, D. B., McBee, M. (2014). *Beyond gifted education: Designing and implementing advanced academic programs.* Waco, TX: Prufrock Press.

Peters, S. J., McBee, M. T., Matthews, M. S., & McCoach, D. B. (2014, March). *Perspectives on the role and relationship between gifted education in research and in K–12 schools.* Paper presented at the Eleventh Biennial Henry B. & Jocelyn Wallace National Research & Policy Symposium on Talent Development. Washington, D.C.

Ricci, M. C. (2013). *Mindsets in the classroom: Building a culture of success and student achievement in schools.* Waco, TX: Prufrock Press.

Szabos, J. (1989). Bright child, gifted learner. *Challenge, 34.* Good Apple.

Note. Adapted from "The Bright vs. Gifted Comparison: A Distraction From What Matters," by S. J. Peters, 2014, *Creativity Post,* retrieved from http://www.creativitypost.com/education/the_bright_vs._gifted_comparison_a_distraction_from_what_matters. Adapted with permission of Scott J. Peters, Ph.D.

Guiding Questions for Small- or Large-Group Discussion

1. What are some of the things that you highlighted in the piece? Why did these sentences have an impact on you?

   _____

   _____

2. The article poses this question: Is the distinction of "bright vs. gifted" educationally helpful?

   _____

   _____

3. Neuroscience tells us that ability/intelligence can be developed—that ability, intelligence, and giftedness are not static. How does this influence our belief system about students who are and are not labeled "gifted"?

   _____

   _____

4. Can you think of any advantages to spending time trying to figure out if a student meets local criteria for "gifted and talented" vs. is just bright? (rather than spending time planning to meet his or her academic needs?)

   _____

   _____

5. In your school or district, is the label "gifted and talented" the only ticket to advanced learning opportunities? Does equitable access exist for all students or only reserved for those who made the cut? What about the bright student who doesn't meet "gifted" criteria but is underchallenged?

   _____

   _____

6. How does a growth mindset belief system contribute to the points made in the article?

   _____

   _____

CHAPTER 8

WHAT ARE SOME WAYS TO HELP STUDENTS ADOPT A GROWTH MINDSET?

The resources in this chapter support students in adopting a growth mindset. A good place to start is finding out what students already know about the brain and teaching students about the role neurons have in learning. More and more studies are surfacing that emphasize the importance of teaching students about their own brains. Increase of motivation, willingness to accept new challenges, and healthier reaction to failure are only a few of the benefits a child will experience when he or she understands how his or her brain works. With tight timelines for curriculum and instruction and school districts' emphasis on consistent educational experiences among grade-level and content-area classes, educators are losing the flexibility to "add on" anything more to an already very crowded curriculum and instruction plan. Therefore creativity is needed when looking for ways to embed some conceptual neuroscience and growth mindset knowledge into instruction.

Keep in mind that many learning experiences must take place over the entire school year—students need to be constantly reminded that they have the ability to get smarter and that each and every brain has an elastic (neuroplasticity) quality to it. It all depends on how you use it. Therefore, we need to be innovative about ways to teach and revisit the concept of malleable intelligence. Begin to think about the subject area and grade level that you teach. Where are the opportunities to introduce some basic brain education and growth mindset concepts?

Several resources are provided in this chapter (additional ideas can be found in Chapter 8 of *Mindsets in the Classroom*) to help students build a conceptual understanding of what happens in the brain when they learn. Some of these resources also help students visualize the neural connections that are made and strengthened with learning, practice, and mastery.

Preassess What Students Already Know About the Brain

Previewing the skills or concepts prior to the preassessment help prime the brain and activate background knowledge. The preassessment preview for elementary students might be as simple as a series of questions that initiate a discussion like the following:

Teacher points to his or her head and says:

⊕ "Who knows what is in here?"

⊕ "What do we use our brain for?"

Teachers will explain to the students that they would like to find out what the students already know about the brain and how it functions. For example, you could say, "I am going to give you a paper, and I would like for you to do two things." Hold up a copy of the blank preassessment for the brain (see Resource 37: Blank Preassessment of Students' Brain Knowledge, p. 89). Ask students to draw a picture of what they think their brains might look like inside the blank outline of the head. Then, students should write down anything that they know about their brain. Remind students that this is not for a grade, but to help you learn what they already know. A preassessment for secondary students might be a written and visual response to this prompt: "Write and illustrate everything you know about the brain." After the students have completed the preassessments, review them, looking for patterns of responses (as illustrated on pages 102–103 in *Mindsets in the Classroom,* some may surprise you), and begin planning for instruction.

Before you implement these learning experiences, give students some background on how the brain works, telling them, "Inside the brain we all have brain cells called neurons. They are so small, we can't see them unless we have very powerful microscope. We have billions of neurons, some connect to each other and some are just sort of floating around." Show them a picture or diagram of a neuron using Resource 38: Neuron Illustration—Primary (younger kids; p. 90) or Resource 39: Neuron Illustration—Secondary (older kids; p. 91). Ask students to talk about anything they notice about the way the neuron looks. Then ask them to think about what might cause these neurons to connect to each other.

Resource 40: Students Become Neurons (pp. 92–93) provides a lesson for teaching students about neurons. It emphasizes what might be happening in the brain when you first learn something new, not understanding yet and not having mastery. I have used this with all ages; in fact, at the high school level, the entire class participated as neurons and they attempted to replicate their teacher's brain.

The Advanced Academics Office including their Primary Talent Development Teachers in Frederick County, MD, took this lesson a step further—they developed the My Connections (see Resource 41, p. 94) graphic to remind students of neural

Blank Preassessment of Students' Brain Knowledge

Draw a picture of what you think your brain looks like.

Write down or ask your teacher to write anything that you know about your brain.

Note. From *Mindsets in the Classroom* (pp. 100) by M. C. Ricci, 2013, Waco, TX: Prufrock Press. Copyright 2013 by Prufrock Press. Reprinted with permission.

Neuron

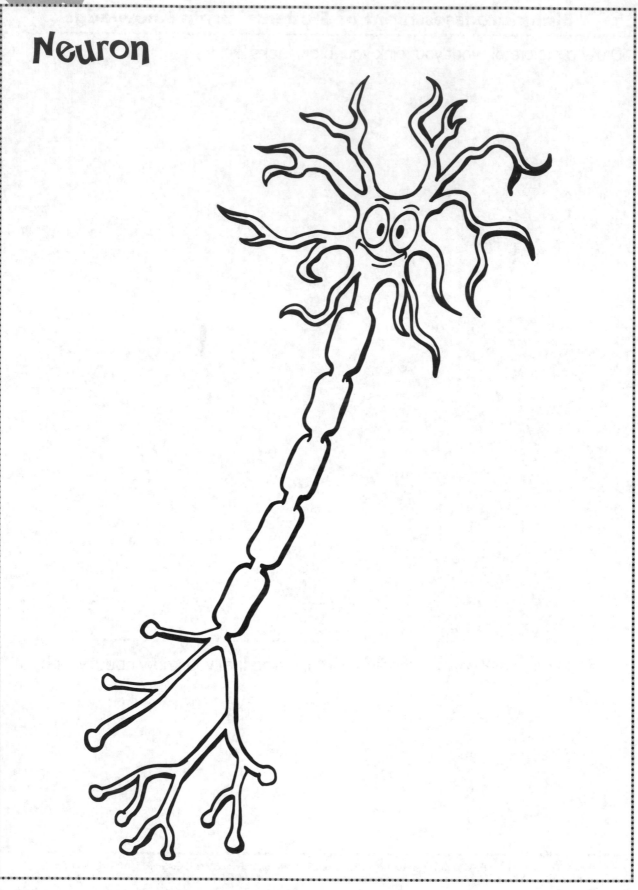

Neuron

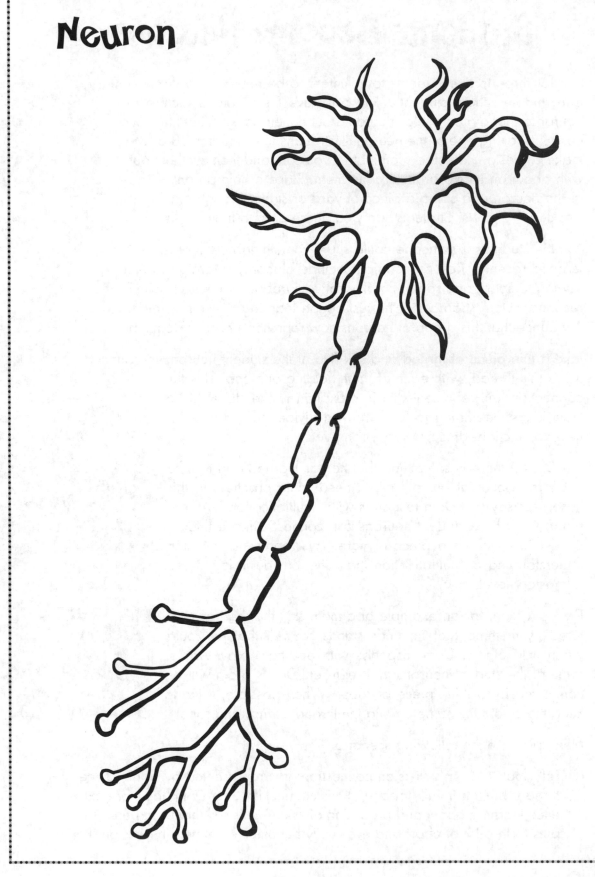

Students Become Neurons

1. Ask for three to five students to volunteer to be neurons. With elementary and middle school students, you can have them hold a picture of a neuron or hang a cardstock neuron around their neck. What I find successful is taking one of the neuron illustrations in Resources 38 or 39, make copies on cardstock, laminate if you can, and then cut them out with about an inch margin around them. Place a hole on any edge of the neuron and string a piece of yard or string through making a "necklace" of sorts. Students can wear these around their necks.

2. Ask the students if someone could share something new that he or she learned recently. Responses might include algebra, a foreign language, sewing, a sport, and so on. For illustrative purposes, we will choose Dom's response. Dom shared that he just began learning division in math class. Announce that this group of neurons now represents part of Dom's brain.

3. Take a thin piece of thread and ask two of the student neurons to connect using this thread, with each of them holding one end. This thin connection will represent division. Explain to the students that Dom is just beginning to learn how to divide, so this is a thin new connection—it is not very strong yet.

4. Ask Dom if there is something that he has learned and that he is getting better at but still might need some practice. In this case, let's say that Dom responds with "multiplication." At that point, two of the student neurons can connect using a thicker connection such as a piece of yarn. This represents a better understanding of multiplication than division, but it is not yet at mastery level.

5. Then ask Dom for an example of a math skill that he has mastered—something that he understands so well that he could teach it to others. Dom responds with addition. Now two or three of the student neurons that represent Dom's brain will be connected by a thick piece of rope. (When possible, I like to keep the colors the same among the thread, string, and rope)

6. Next, propose the following scenario:

   a. Let's look at Dom's division connection: It is represented by a thin piece of thread, but what will happen to this connection after Dom has more experience learning about and practicing division? Let's say that Dom persists and puts forth a lot of effort and eventually becomes an expert in division. How

 Ready-to-Use Resources for Mindsets in the Classroom © Prufrock Press Inc.

will this connection change? At this point demonstrate how this thread of a connection is replaced with a strong, thick rope.

b. What if, instead, Dom decides that division is just too hard for him and he gives up? What will happen to this connection? (It will remain a "not yet" connection or disconnect entirely.)

c. Think about this: When Dom is on summer vacation he does not practice his division skills at all. On the first day of school he is given a preassessment to see what he remembers about math. What do you think might have happened to his division connections? (They got thinner because they were not used.) They will strengthen a lot quicker since the learning is not completely new. He just has to practice.

7. Ask students to think of a time when they felt frustrated learning something new. Ask them to visualize their neurons making stronger connections every time they push through the challenge and master new learning. Tell them to think about these neural connections when they are faced with a challenge. Remind them, "Once you build a strong connection, you have added density to your brain and actually made yourself smarter!"

8. Introduce the charts you will hang in the room: My Connections (Resource 41) and How Will Your Brain Grow and Learn Today (Resource 42)? You can also make copies for all of the students to keep on their desk, or inside their agenda book.

9. A suggested next step is asking students to complete My Strong and "Not Yet" Neural Connections (Resource 43).

My Connections . . .

New

Not yet . . .

Strong

I try, I practice, I GROW!

connections in their brain. This chart can be displayed and referred to as students are learning as a continuous reminder of strengthening neural connections. They also developed a visual called "How Will Your Brain Learn and Grow Today?" (see Resource 42, p. 96) This visual is another way to remind students of the different stages of neural connectivity.

Reflecting on Their Own Learning

Ask students to think about skills they have recently learned as well as things they have known for a long time and understand fully. Using Resource 43: My Strong and "Not Yet" Neural Connections (p. 97), ask students to draw their strong and "not yet" neural connections. Ask students to think about things they understand and are very good at as well as things that they are just learning, but "not yet" understanding fully. The new learning will be represented by a very thin or dotted line, the "not yet" learning should be represented by a thicker line, and mastery learning should be represented by a very thick line between the neurons. (You may want to refer to Resource 42 to demonstrate this idea of the connections grower "thicker.") Older students typically fill up the brain with many connections. Remind younger students to draw their neurons small (they don't have to actually look like neurons) so that they can fit many connections in their brain. This is an interesting task to do quarterly so that they can compare their brain growth over time.

"Yet"

The power of *yet* has become very prevalent in education recently, between Carol Dweck's On the Power of Yet (https://www.youtube.com/watch?v=ZyAde4nIIm8) and Sesame Street's Power of Yet song (https://www.youtube.com/watch?v=X LeUvZvuvAs), I have seen that educators, parents, and coaches are embracing the importance of the word "yet." In fact, in several middle and high school classrooms I visited, I noticed the word "yet" in big letters hanging on the classroom wall as a reminder. Resource 44 (p. 100) is a sample lesson (that was inspired by Frederick County, MD's, Advanced Academics Office) that could be used to talk with students about the power of the word "yet." Resource 45 (p. 101) is a diagram that demonstrates how neurons and connections grow as students learn more—it illustrates the amount of growth that occurs between birth and age 7. This can be used within the context of the Power of Yet lesson or independent of the lesson

How will your brain learn and grow today?

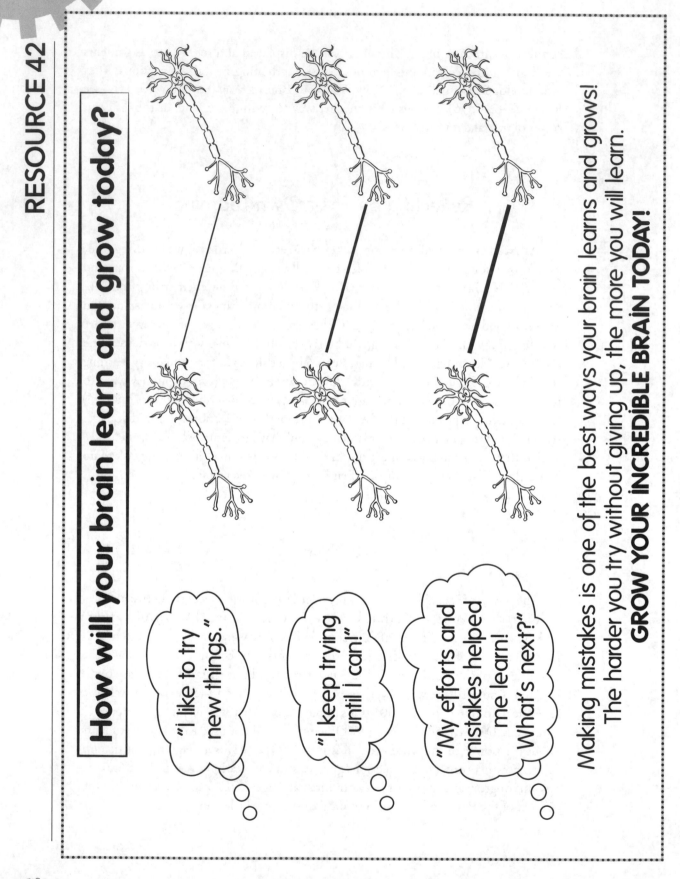

"I like to try new things."

"I keep trying until I can!"

"My efforts and mistakes helped me learn! What's next?"

Making mistakes is one of the best ways your brain learns and grows! The harder you try without giving up, the more you will learn. **GROW YOUR INCREDIBLE BRAIN TODAY!**

My Strong and "Not Yet" Neural Connections

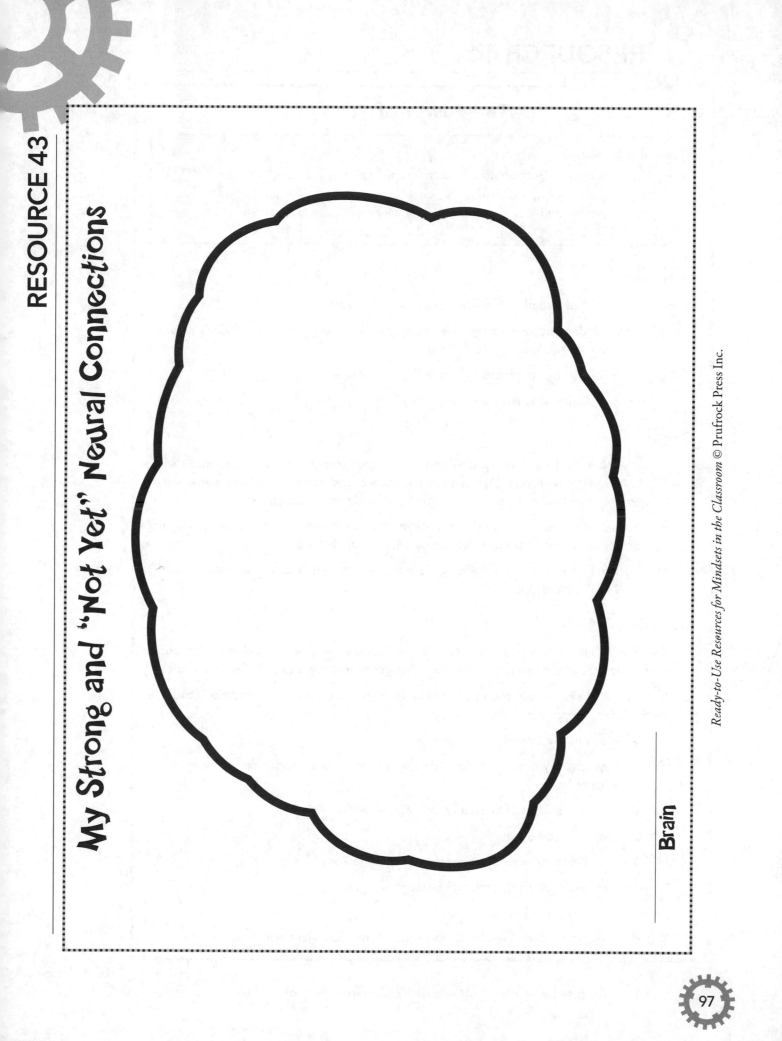

Brain

Ready-to-Use Resources for Mindsets in the Classroom © Prufrock Press Inc.

The Power of Yet

Teacher's Notes:

➢ Use after students participate in and understand the neuron lesson in Resource 40.

➢ Even though part of this learning experience is based on a picture book, it provides a powerful metaphor for taking on many new challenges—it could really be used at all grade levels.

Materials

➢ a full spool of thread or a full ball of thin string or yarn

➢ book that demonstrates someone learning something new such as *Walk On! A Guide for Babies of All Ages* by Marla Frazee

➢ picture of neurons at birth and at age 7 (see Resource 45)

➢ a poster or sign with the word "yet"

Goals

➢ To explain that the brain grows and makes connections through experiences such as learning new things, struggling to understand, taking on challenges, persevering, learning from mistakes, trying new strategies, and putting forth effort.

➢ Students will understand and communicate that the harder we try without giving up (persevering) and sticking with something (stamina), the more we learn.

➢ Teacher and students will demonstrate how we can turn "I can't" statements into "I can't *yet!*" statements.

Instructions

1. Share this goal with the students: "Today we will review what we learned about the brain and explore how to make our connections stronger so that our brain can learn and grow."

2. Show a picture of a neuron and ask the students to share what they remember about it. Students may respond with the following:

   O Neurons are everywhere in your brain.

   O They are tiny brain cells that make signals to send messages that tell your body what to do.

   O You have billions of these in your brain.

   O They are really, really tiny.

   O They help you learn by connecting to other neurons.

   O Your brain grows by making connections.

If students do not mention the above, share the information with them.

 Ready-to-Use Resources for Mindsets in the Classroom © Prufrock Press Inc.

3. Show students the picture of the neurons at birth and then of a 7-year-old. Use Resource 45 to display this.

4. Ask them what they notice in the illustration. Point out that the 7-year-old brain has more neural connections and is denser—ask them why they think this is.

5. Choose a book or piece of text that centers around learning something new. For illustrative purposes, this lesson will use *Walk On! A Guide for Babies of All Ages* by Marla Frazee

6. Share with students a time when you had to learn to do something new (e.g., tried a new cooking technique, tried to learn your way around a new city or country, practiced a new sport, learned to skate, learned a new language, etc.). Share your story and emphasize the roadblocks and struggles that you encountered along the way (e.g., fears, failures, support you needed to find, new strategies you had to use).

7. Share with students that you found a book that reminds you of your own experience. Ask students: *Do you remember what I had to do to make those connections stronger?* (Find support, make mistakes, persevere, build my stamina, practice, try new strategies, set smaller goals, etc.) Listen to this story and see how the baby reacts and what he or she has to do as he or she learns something new. (Have the three sizes of string/rope and two neurons visible in case students want to refer to them during the book discussion.)

8. Read the book in its entirety once, then ask: *Can the steps that the baby took be applied to learning to do anything?* Read the book again, stopping at the following places in the book for discussion and reflection.

Quote From the Book	Question to Pose
"You will need support. This is tricky because sometimes what you think will support you won't."	Think of a time when you wanted to try something new and you realized that you might need some kind of support from other people. Let's share some of those experiences.
"Now. Get a grip. Pull yourself up, stand."	How do you interpret the phrases "Get a grip" and "Pull yourself up"? What can these be applied to other than learning to walk?
"Are your knees buckling? That's okay."	When you learn something new, do you sometimes face challenge or a setback? How does that relate to the baby's knees buckling, and why is it okay?
"It may take some time, remember to breathe."	What does "remember to breathe mean"? Why is it important?
"Oops. It is very common to fall down."	What does this statement mean?
"You can try again, but first, run down the checklist."	What is on the baby's checklist? Why is this important?
"Look toward where you want to go."	How does this relate to something new that you are learning? (Mention a specific example of something they are learning in your class.)
"Take the first step. And another and another. It gets easier, huh?"	Why does it get easier? How does this baby's story relate to perseverance and resiliency? What would happen if babies gave up on learning to walk?

You may also want to discuss more deeply about all that the baby did in the story to make his or her connections strong for walking (find support, make mistakes, persevere, build my stamina, practice, try new strategies, set smaller goals, etc.).

9. Write on chart paper, smart board, sentence strip, or the board the following: "I can't _____." Tell the students there are some things that we just aren't so good at; we haven't developed those strong connections. Complete the sentence with something you can't do such as "I can't swim." Go back to the sentence and add the word "yet," so it becomes "I can't swim yet."

10. Ask the students think of something that they aren't good at **yet**. Have them stand or sit in a circle on the floor and tell them that they are now all neurons in a brain. (If students have their paper neuron "necklaces," they should put them on.) Each student will take turns and complete this sentence, "I can't _____ yet!" After they say the sentence, they will roll a spool of thread or ball of string/yarn to another student. Be sure to tell them to hold the end of the string with one hand while they roll the spool or ball of string with the other hand.

11. When everyone has had a turn, ask students to hold their connection and stand if they were sitting on the floor. Point out that all of these connection are "not yet" connections and when they do all of the things that the baby did—find support, balance, time, courage, resiliency, strategy, a path, practice, and perseverance—then the connections will get stronger.

Closure

1. Create a simple poster with the word yet in all capitals. Show this to students. Let students know that we all have things that we aren't good at yet, but if they practice, have determination, and persevere they will eventually accomplish their goal.

2. You may also give students a blank index card and ask them to write the word "yet" on it. They can tape it to the corner of their desk or workspace as a reminder.

3. Or, you could close with Sesame Street's Power of Yet song/video (sung by Janelle Monae, found at https://www.youtube.com/watch?v=XLeUvZvuvAs).

Diagram of How Neurons Change From Birth to Age 7

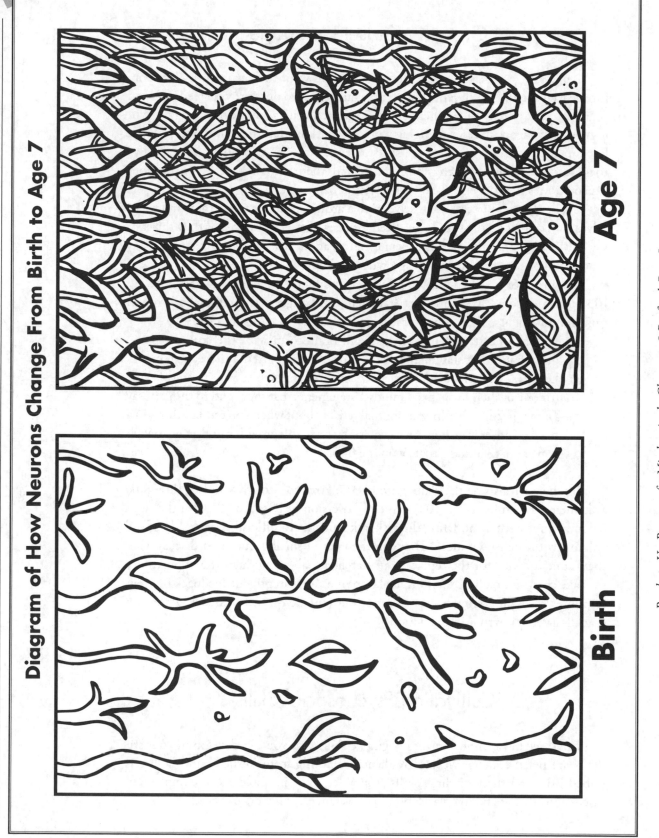

Age 7

Birth

Ready-to-Use Resources for Mindsets in the Classroom © Prufrock Press Inc.

Growth Mindset Language

Deliberate instruction about the language you want to hear in your classroom is time well spent. Let students know that your goal is to only provide feedback and praise in a way that values their effort, strategies, critical thinking, struggle, willingness to take on more challenging work, the actions that they take, and so forth. Explain that telling them they are smart, clever, creative, or brilliant, doesn't give them feedback about what they have done, it tells them who they are. Share that your expectation is that they speak to each other the same way.

Challenge them to talk themselves into a growth mindset when they find themselves thinking or saying things in a fixed mindset way. For example, if they think or say "This is too hard for me," ask them for ideas about what they could think or say that would be more aligned with a growth mindset.

Resource 46: Fixed to Growth Mindset Thoughts/Statements for Students (p. 103) provides some fixed mindset statements and suggested replacement growth mindset statements. There are several ways that you can use this resource:

⚙ Present one statement each day and brainstorm with the students some growth mindset statements that could replace the fixed mindset statement.

⚙ Use these statements for journal writing. Ask students to choose one of these (or one of their own) fixed mindset statements that they tend to think or say. Then tell students, "In your journal reflect about when you tend to think in a fixed mindset way, then set a goal for reacting in a growth mindset way when you are in a similar situation in the future."

Teachers can also use the blank Resource 47: Fixed to Growth Mindset Thoughts/ Statements for Students (p. 104), which is a version of Resource 47 with the right column empty. After modeling the task, ask students to fill in the right side of the column with their own ideas. They can then get in small groups and discuss what they came up with for the replacement statement, allowing them the opportunity to make changes or adjust their original response. You can provide feedback on their responses through comments, but do not put a grade on it. (Feedback without a grade is a very growth mindset action!)

Cultivating Psychosocial Skills

The three most important noncognitive skills that you can develop in your students are perseverance, grit, and resiliency. Learning from mistakes and failure is imbedded in all three of these skills. The video links in Table 1 can complement discussions that are taking place about perseverance, resiliency, and grit.

Fixed to Growth Mindset Thoughts/ Statements for Students

Possible ways to use these thoughts/statements:

➢ Present one statement each day and brainstorm with the students some growth mindset statements that could replace the fixed mindset statement.

➢ Use these statements for journal writing. Ask students to choose one of these (or one of their own) fixed mindset statements that they tend to think or say. Then tell students, "In your journal reflect about when you tend to think in a fixed mindset way, then set a goal for reacting in a growth mindset way when you are in a similar situation in the future."

Fixed Mindset Statement	Possible Growth Mindset Replacement Statements
I am never going to understand this!	➢ I need to change my strategy or the way I approach this. ➢ What question can I ask (e.g., of the teacher, Google, etc.) that may help me understand?
This is so easy for me.	➢ I wonder what I can do to make this more challenging? ➢ Even though I think this is easy, I need to think carefully about it so I understand it completely.
I am not good at this.	➢ I am not good at this yet but if I keep practicing or try a different strategy, I know I will improve.
She is the smart one; I will never be like her.	➢ If I consistently put forth effort, I know that I will have more success. ➢ Her neurons must have strong connections; I need to get my neurons going!
I am really good in art.	➢ I need to continue to work on my technique in art so that I will improve.
Math is just not my thing.	➢ I need to put more time into practicing these math concepts. ➢ My neurons are not connecting in math yet, so I need to figure out some ways that will help.
Ugh! I keep messing up!	➢ That was an epic failure! What can I learn from it for my next try?
I have a green thumb.	➢ Learning about and experimenting with growing things has really helped me have success.

Fixed to Growth Mindset Thoughts/ Statements for Students

Name:_____ Date:_____

Fixed Mindset Statement	Possible Growth Mindset Replacement Statements
I am never going to understand this!	
This is so easy for me.	
I am not good at this.	
She is the smart one; I will never be like her.	
I am really good in art.	
Math is just not my thing.	
Ugh! I keep messing up!	
I have a green thumb.	

TABLE 1

VIDEOS FOR DISCUSSING PERSEVERANCE, RESILIENCY, AND GRIT

Name of Video	Link	Grade Level	Length
Resilience Animation	https://www.youtube.com/watch?v=C1UCl2ZHEqw	4–12	3.43
Sesame Street: Bruno Mars: Don't Give Up (perseverance)	https://www.youtube.com/watch?v=pWp6kkz-pnQ	PreK–3	1.57
Powerful Inspirational True Story . . . Don't Give Up! (resiliency)	https://www.youtube.com/watch?v=kZlXWp6vFdE	2–12	3.14
Perseverance. The Story of Nick Vujicic	https://www.youtube.com/watch?v=gNnVdlvodTQ	4–12	3.37

Literature

One of the most effective ways to keep the growth mindset discussion going all year long is through literature. After reading many, many, many books, I have compiled a list of picture books as well as extended texts (term used loosely) that provide opportunities for discussions about mindsets. Resource 48: Growth Mindset Picture Books (pp. 106–112) provides a list of picture books and Resource 49: Growth Mindset Extended Texts (pp. 113–117) provides a list of extended texts along with the author, recommended grade level (although I am a fan of using picture books at every level), date published, and whether the character or story demonstrates a fixed mindset, growth mindset, or both. I also added a column that refers to any evidence from the story that supports the mindset. The inclusion of some growth mindset questions that could be asked about the text rounds out the table. Many question possibilities exist for each book—these are just a few examples of questions in order to begin a discussion about mindsets.

A growth mindset poster that can be hung in every classroom and hallway as a trigger for thinking about having a growth mindset is included as Resource 50: Growth Mindset Poster (p. 118).

Growth Mindset Picture Books

Book or Story	Author	Grade Level	Year Published	Character(s)	Fixed, Growth, or Both?	Evidence From Text	Mindset Question
A Little Bit of Oomph	Barney Saltzberg	PreK–5	2013	N/A	Growth	Oomph is effort. The book shows what can happen with a little bit of effort.	What does "oomph" mean? Why does the author think that the things in the book (like seeds) need a little oomph? Why is oomph important for a growth mindset?
All the Way to America: The Story of a Big Italian Family and a Little Shovel	Dan Yaccarino	K–3	2014	Michael, Dan, Mike, Dan	Growth	Each generation of the family worked hard and persevered to take care of their family.	What is the same about each generation of this family (they all worked hard)? What do you think the little shovel might symbolize?
Allie's Basketball Dream	Barbara Barber	K–3	2013	Allie	Growth	Allie wants to learn to play basketball even though the boys tell her it is not a girl's game. She practices her skills. She is determined to play well.	Why did the other kids discourage Allie from playing basketball? What is their mindset?
Almost	Richard Torrey	PreK–3	2009	Jack	Growth	Jack can "almost" do a lot of things.	In our class, we like to use the word "yet", how is the word "almost" the same or different from the word "yet?"
Amazing Grace	Mary Hoffman	PreK–3	1991	Grace	Growth	Grace was determined to play Peter Pan so she practiced all weekend.	Which characters in the book demonstrated a fixed mindset?
Barefoot: Escape on the Underground Railroad	Pamela Duncan Edwards	1–4	1998	Barefoot	Growth	Barefoot must elude the men in heavy boots. He perseveres until he finds a safe haven.	What roles do the animals play? What was Barefoot running away from? Would a slave have success on the underground railroad if he or she had a fixed mindset? Why?
Beautiful Oops	Barney Saltzberg	PreK–3	2010	N/A	Growth	A torn piece of paper, a spill, these are things to celebrate and provide new opportunities!	Why did the author write this book? What can we learn about mistakes after reading this? What are some ways that we can turn a mistake into something positive?
Blizzard	John Rocco	K–3	2014	Boy	Growth	The boy walked through snow with tennis rackets on his feet to try to get to the market.	Why does the boy say, "It was a perilous journey"? What are some words that describe the boy?

Ready-to-Use Resources for Mindsets in the Classroom © Prufrock Press Inc.

106

Book or Story	Author	Grade Level	Year Published	Character(s)	Fixed, Growth, or Both?	Evidence From Text	Mindset Question
Brave Irene	William Steig	PreK–3	2011	Irene	Growth	Irene persevered through wind, snow, a heavy box, a twisted ankle, and nightfall.	Irene asked herself, "How long a small person could keep this struggle up" . . . what does she mean by this statement?
Butterflies for Kiri	Cathlyn Falwell	K–3	2003	Kiri	Growth	Kiri practiced and persevered until she was successful with origami.	While Kiri was learning origami, what strategy did she use so that she would not waste the beautiful paper? Citing evidence from the text, did Kiri have a growth or fixed mindset?
Cartwheel Katie	Fran Manushkin	PreK–2	2015	Katie	Both	Katie said "It's hard when it's not easy" and "I don't like cartwheels," but Katie practiced and kept trying.	Katie had to really practice to improve. Have you ever had to to practice hard to learn something? When does Katie demonstrate a fixed mindset? What made her change to a growth mindset?
The Curious Garden	Peter Brown	K–3	2009	Liam	Growth	Liam worked hard transforming an old elevated railroad track into a beautiful garden.	Why did Liam work so hard on the garden? Why do you think the author chose *The Curious Garden* for the title? What kind of mindset does Liam have? Use evidence from the text to support your answer.
Dear Benjamin Banneker	Andrea Davis Pinkney	1–4	1994	Benjamin	Growth	Benjamin demonstrated a strong work ethic. He became an astronomer and published an almanac. He took a stand against slavery and shared his thoughts with Thomas Jefferson.	What parts of the story demonstrate Benjamin's growth mindset?
The Dot	Peter H. Reynolds	PreK–3	2003	Vashti	Fixed, then growth	Vashti said "I just can't draw!" (fixed mindset statement). Thanks to the growth mindset of her teacher, she began to show growth in her artwork.	Why did the teacher ask Vashti to sign her artwork? How did that change Vashti's mindset?
Dream Big, Little Pig!	Kristi Yamaguchi	PreK–2	2011	Poppy	Growth	Poppy finally puts time and effort into something she want to do, ice skating, and she has success.	Poppy dreams about being a dancer, singer, and a model. What stands in her way of reaching these dreams (practice, effort)? Why does Poppy finally succeed in learning to ice skate?

Ready-to-Use Resources for Mindsets in the Classroom © Prufrock Press Inc.

Book or Story	Author	Grade Level	Year Published	Character(s)	Fixed, Growth, or Both?	Evidence From Text	Mindset Question
Everyone Can Learn to Ride a Bicycle	Chris Raschka	PreK–3	2013	The child	Growth	The child tries many things and perseveres.	What are some of the things that the child tried when she was learning to ride the bike? What are some words that describe the child?
Flight School	Lita Judge	PreK–3	2014	Penguin	Growth	A persevering penguin is determined to learn how to fly.	Why does the penguin want to fly? Why doesn't he just give up? What is his mindset?
Giraffes Can't Dance	Giles Andreae	PreK–K	2001	Gerald	Both	Gerald gave up before he tried to dance, then Cricket had him approach dancing in a different way.	Why did Gerald change his mind about his own dancing abilities?
The Girl Who Never Made Mistakes	Mark Pett and Gary Rubinstein	K–3	2011	Beatrice	Fixed, then growth	Fixed: She never wanted to make a mistake and she did not take risks (ice skating) for fear of failure. Growth: She learned that making mistakes is more fun and interesting	Why didn't Beatrice want to make a mistake? What did she learn after she made her big mistake at the talent show? Why do you think her brother Carl loved to make mistakes?
Going Places	Peter and Paul Reynolds	PreK–3	2014	Rafael and Maya	Growth	Maya thought about all of the possibilities for her go-cart. She never thought, "I can't do this."	Why did Maya choose to make something different? Why do you think that Rafael wanted to collaborate?
Grace for President	Kelly S. DiPucchio	1–3	2012	Grace	Growth	Grace is running for school president. She demonstrates determination and persistence.	Why didn't Thomas campaign as much as Grace did? What is Thomas's mindset?
I Can Be Anything	Jerry Spinelli	PreK–1	2010	Boy	Growth	The boy believes that he can be anything he wants to be when he grows up.	Why does the boy think that he can be anything? What is his mindset? What will he need to do to become one of these things (practice, persevere)?
If You Want to See a Whale	Julie Fogliano	PreK–2	2013	Boy	Growth	The boy demonstrates persistence and perseverance as he waits to see a whale.	Why do you think the boy waits and waits and waits to see a whale? What are some words that describe him?
Iggy Peck Architect	Andrea Beaty	PreK–3	2007	Iggy and Lila Greer	Iggy = Growth; Lila = Fixed	Iggy wanted to build everything out of anything. Lila did not want any building to occur in her classroom. She said, "It had no place in grade 2."	Why didn't everyone appreciate Iggy's growth mindset?

Ready-to-Use Resources for Mindsets in the Classroom © Prufrock Press Inc.

Book or Story	Author	Grade Level	Year Published	Character(s)	Fixed, Growth, or Both?	Evidence From Text	Mindset Question
The Imaginary Garden	Andrew Larsen	PreK–3	2009	Theo and Poppa	Growth	Poppa was unable to grow his garden in his new apartment so Theo and Poppa decided to create an imaginary garden.	Why didn't Poppa just say, "We can't have a garden here"? Describe Theo and Poppa's mindsets.
It's OK to Make Mistakes	Todd Parr	PreK–K	2014	N/A	Growth	All the characters in this story remind the reader that it is OK to make mistakes. You can fix it, learn something from it, or discover something new each time.	What kinds of mindset do all of the characters in this book have? Give examples from the book. Think of a mistake that you have made; what can you learn from it?
Knots on a Counting Rope	Bill Martin Jr. and John Archambault	1–4	1987	Boy-Strength-of-Blue-Horses	Growth	The boy was born blind, but learned many things through perseverance and optimism.	What do the knots on the counting rope symbolize? What does grandfather mean when he says, "Dark mountains are always around us. They have no beginnings and they have no endings"? What are some ways that both the grandfather and the boy demonstrate a growth mindset?
The Little Engine That Could	Watty Piper	PreK–2	1930	Little Engine	Growth	The Little Engine shows perseverance, states "I think I can" until it has success.	Why does the Little Engine think it can go up the hill? Why doesn't the Little Engine just give up?
Making a Splash	Carol E. Riley	PreK–4	2015	Lisa and Johnny	Lisa = Growth; Johnny = Fixed	Johnny is so successful using the kickboard that he does not want to learn to swim without it. He is afraid of failure. Lisa works hard to overcome her struggle and eventually learns how to swim.	What did Lisa do when she felt herself sinking? What did she learn from this?
The Most Magnificent Thing	Ashley Spires	PreK–3	2014	Girl	Growth	The girl perseveres until she has built the most magnificent thing.	Why didn't the little girl just give up? How would you describe the little girl?
Odd Boy Out: Young Albert Einstein	Don Brown	PreK–3	2008	Albert	Growth	Albert practices violin, he taught himself geometry, he embraces challenging math problems, and he perseveres after being rejected from a college.	Why did Albert's teacher tell him that he will "never get anywhere in life"? What are some ways that Albert demonstrated a growth mindset?

Ready-to-Use Resources for Mindsets in the Classroom © Prufrock Press Inc.

Book or Story	Author	Grade Level	Year Published	Character(s)	Fixed, Growth, or Both?	Evidence From Text	Mindset Question
The OK Book	Amy Krouse Rosenthal	PreK–3	2007	OK	Growth	OK states that he is "OK" at a lot of things. He tries a lot of different things.	What will OK need to do in order to "Grow up to be really excellent at something" (practice, demonstrate resiliency, persevere)?
The Pout Pout Fish Goes to School	Deborah Diesen	PreK–K	2014	Mr. Fish	Fixed, then growth = Mr Fish; Growth = Miss Hewitt	Mr. Fish believes that he is not smart, he will never get it, he doesn't belong, and he wants to forget it. His teacher. Miss Hewitt, states, "You don't have to know things that you haven't learned yet" and "With practice, you will get it."	Why does Mr. Fish list all of his troubles when he doesn't have success? What does he have to do in order to have success? What is his mindset? What is Miss Hewitt's mindset?
Prudence Wants a Pet	Cathleen Daly	PreK–3	2011	Prudence	Growth	Prudence is persistent in trying to get a pet. She tries a branch, a twig, an old shoe, her brother, and a tire.	Why did Prudence choose things as pets? What words describe Prudence (persistent)?
Rosie Revere, Engineer	Andrea Beaty	K–3	2013	Rosie and Great, Great Aunt Rose	Aunt Rose = Growth	"Your brilliant first flop was a raging success. Come on, let's get busy and on to the next."	Why did the children stand and cheer at each failure?
Ruby's Wish	Shirin Yim Bridges	PreK–3	2002	Ruby	Growth	Ruby studies very hard and wants to go to university, but only boys are allowed to go.	Why did Ruby's grandfather allow her to attend university? What was his mindset?
Scaredy Squirrel	Melanie Watt	PreK–3	2008	Scaredy	Both	Scaredy will not leave his tree, as he is afraid or the unknown (fixed mindset). Scaredy is suddenly out of his tree and he begins to look at things differently (growth mindset).	What happened that allowed Scaredy's mindset to change?
Snowflake Bentley	Jacqueline Briggs Martin	K–4	2009	Willie	Growth	Day after day, Willie studied ice crystals. For three winters, he tried drawing snow crystals. He was resilient after many attemps with the camera.	What are some words that describe Willie? Refer back to the text and identify parts that demonstrated his growth mindset.
Someday	Eileen Spinelli	PreK–3	2007	Little girl	Growth	The little girl talks about her future goals and what she is doing right now to prepare for them.	What kinds of things is the little girl doing to prepare for the things she wants to do someday? What are some things that you want to do someday? What can you do now to prepare?

Ready-to-Use Resources for Mindsets in the Classroom © Prufrock Press Inc.

Book or Story	Author	Grade Level	Year Published	Character(s)	Fixed, Growth, or Both?	Evidence From Text	Mindset Question
Stand Tall, Molly Lou Melon	Patty Lovell	PreK–3	2001	Molly Lou Melon and Grandma	Growth	Thanks to Grandma's advice, Molly Lou Melon made the best of every situation.	Why was Molly Lou Melon so optimistic? Do you think you would react the same way if you were faced with the same things that Molly Lou was?
Stuck	Oliver Jeffers	PreK–2	2011	Floyd	Growth	Floyd tried everything he could think of to get his kite unstuck. He persevered.	Why didn't Floyd just give up?
Thank You, Mr. Falker	Patricia Polacco	K–3	1998	Trisha	Fixed, then growth	Trisha could not read. She found ways to make it appear as if she could, but she gave up trying. Mr. Falker became her teacher in fifth grade and realized that Trisha did not see letters and numbers the same way as everyone else. Trisha persevered and practiced until she could read.	Citing evidence from the book, what are some ways that Trisha had a fixed mindset? What did she eventually have to do to learn to read?
Thanks for the Feedback, I Think.	Julia Cook	K–3	2013	RJ	Fixed, then growth	RJ doesn't know how to respond to feedback. When Sam gives him feedback about soccer, RJ says, "What do you know about shooting?"	Show the students the picture on page 20. Ask students the following: What do you see in this picture? Why does RJ's dad tell him that feedback is a good thing? How is feedback information that helps you grow?
The Tin Forest	Helen Ward	PreK–2	2003	The Old Man	Growth	The old man had an idea to turn the garbage into a forest. His idea grew and grew until he had a forest of tin.	The old man had hope and dreams of a real forest. Do you think that the birds would have come if he hadn't built a tin forest? Explain your thinking.
The Tortoise & the Hare	Jerry Pinkney (based on Aesop's fable)	PreK–3	2013	Tortoise and Hare	Both	Hare is so sure of his innate talents, he takes it easy. Tortoise perseveres.	Referring back to the text, describe the mindset of both Tortoise and Hare.
Walk On! A Guide for Babies of All Ages	Marla Frazee	PreK–3	2006	Baby	Growth	Baby needs support, balance, time, courage, resiliency, strategy, a path, practice, and perseverance.	How is learning to walk the same as learning with a growth mindset?

Ready-to-Use Resources for Mindsets in the Classroom © Prufrock Press Inc.

Book or Story	Author	Grade Level	Year Published	Character(s)	Fixed, Growth, or Both?	Evidence From Text	Mindset Question
What Do You Do With an Idea?	Kobi Yamada	PreK–3	2014	The little boy	Fixed, then growth	"I actually thought about giving up on my idea" (fixed). "I liked being with my ideas. It made me feel more alive, like I could do anything." (growth)	Why was the boy hesitant about sharing his idea? How did the boy feel when people thought his idea was silly? Once he realized that it was his crazy idea, how did he change?
When Pigs Fly	Valerie Coulman	PreK–2	2003	Ralph	Growth	Ralph is determined to get a bike even though cows don't ride bikes.	In what ways does Ralph demonstrate a growth mindset?
Who Says Women Can't be Doctors?	Tanya Lee Stone	K–3	2013	Elizabeth Blackwell	Growth	Elizabeth refused to accept that people believed that women weren't smart enough to be doctors. She does not take no for an answer.	How did Elizabeth's growth mindset help more women become doctors?
Wilma Unlimited	Kathleen Krull	1–4	2000	Wilma Rudolph	Growth	Wilma overcame health issues and eventually earned an Olympic medal.	What are some ways that Wilma persevered through her hardships?

Ready-to-Use Resources for Mindsets in the Classroom © Prufrock Press Inc.

Growth Mindset Extended Texts

Book or Story	Author	Grade Level	Year Published	Character(s)	Fixed, Growth, or Both?	Evidence From Text	Mindset Question
A Long Walk to Water	Linda Sue Park	5–9	2011	Salva	Both	Salva perseveres after being separated from his family through the desert of Sudan, war, hunger, thirst, crocodiles, gunfire, mosquitos, etc.	When Salva feels like giving up in the desert, his uncle gives him small goals, such as a rock or another landmark. After he successfully reaches each goal, he is given another. How is that kind of goal setting the same or different from your own goal setting? How would Salva's experience and journey be different if he had a fixed mindset?
The Blossoming Universe of Violet Diamond	Brenda Woods	4–7	2015	Violet, Mom, Bibi	Growth	"I practiced over and over again until finally one day I did" (p. 27). "I wished I could be a doctor, but then I worked hard to make that wish come true" (p. 26). "There is always room for improvement" (p. 30). "I've worked very hard to make it a nop-notch unit" (p. 93). "Persistence definitely runs in the family" (p. 174).	Violet wishes for things. What needs to happen with a wish in order to have a growth mindset?
The Cay	Theodore Taylor	7–10	1969	Timothy and Philip	Timothy = Growth; Philip = both	Timothy demonstrated optimism when they were on the raft. Philip demonstrated a growth mindset as he learned to work on the island.	Describe Philip's mindset on the raft and then after Timothy died. How would the story be different if Philip kept a fixed mindset?
Chains	Laurie Halse Anderson	5–10	2008	Isabel	Growth	Isabel demonstrated resilience throughout all the hardships that she faced.	Using evidence from the text, describe Isabel's mindset. Did any of the other characters demonstrate a growth mindset? Why was Isabel so resilient?
Charlie and the Chocolate Factory	Roald Dahl	3	1964	Charlie	Growth	Charlie kept buying chocolate, never gave up, and was optimistic.	Did Willy Wonka have a growth mindset, fixed mindset, or both? Cite evidence from the text.

Ready-to-Use Resources for Mindsets in the Classroom © Prufrock Press Inc.

Book or Story	Author	Grade Level	Year Published	Character(s)	Fixed, Growth, or Both?	Evidence From Text	Mindset Question
Counting by 7's	Holly Goldberg Sloan	5–8	2014	Willow	Both	Willow persevered in all that she was interested in. She also told Jairo, "Never let someone tell you that you can't do it" (p. 94).	When Willow learns that she is "highly gifted" she states, "It's possible that all labels are curses. Unless they are on cleaning products" (p. 18). What does she mean by this? How could this relate to our discussion of mindsets?
Fluter: The Story of Four Sisters and an Incredible Journey	Erin E. Moulton	3–5	2012	Maple	Growth	This story is a good example of when having a growth mindset results in a poor decision. Maple persists in finding "miracle" water for her premature baby sister and goes on a dangerous journey to find it.	Maple and Dawn demonstrate a growth mindset when they are on their journey. Did they make the right decision? What are some other examples of when having a growth mindset might lead to a dangerous situation?
Gifted Hands: The Ben Carson Story (Revised Kids' Edition)	Greg and Deborah Shaw Lewis	3	2009	Ben and Ben's mom	Growth	"That day Ben made up his mind to keep reading until he was the smartest kid in his class—just like his mother said he could be" (p. 30).	What do you think might have happened to Ben if he had a fixed mindset about his abilities?
Good Night, Mr. Tom	Michelle Magorian	6–10	1986	Mr. Tom	Growth	Mr. Tom believed that William could become stronger, learn to read, and grow in many ways.	What was Mr. Tom's mindset when he first met William? Would you describe him as an optimist or a pessimist? Explain why.
Holes	Louis Sachar	4–6	2000	Warden, Mr. Sir, Mr. Pendanski	Fixed	They don't think the boys will ever amount to anything.	In some ways, the adults had a growth mindset—they were determined to find the treasure and the Warden was willing to have the boys dig for years until the treasure was found. Give examples of the fixed mindset behaviors that the adults exhibited. How is it possible to have both a fixed and growth mindset?
I Funny: A Middle School Story	James Patterson	4–7	2013	Jamie Grimm	Both	"Jamie practiced all over Long Beach" (p. 146). "You worked hard, you never gave up" (p. 191).	Do you agree that Jamie's mindset fluctuated? What are some of the reasons? Most of the time, did he have a fixed or growth mindset?

Ready-to-Use Resources for Mindsets in the Classroom © Prufrock Press Inc.

114

Book or Story	Author	Grade Level	Year Published	Character(s)	Fixed, Growth, or Both?	Evidence From Text	Mindset Question
May B	Caroline Starr Rose	4–7	2012	Mavis "May"	Both	"I am Mavis Elizabeth Betterly. I am used to hard work. I can run a household better that Mrs. Oblinger ever could" and "What does it matter when I make mistakes? They don't make me who I am" (p. 161).	May B was put in a position where she had to persevere in order to survive. Describe some of the times where she almost gave up. Why did she keep going?
The Miraculous Journey of Edward Tulane	Kate DiCamillo	2–5	2009	Edward	Both	Perseveres through several "owners" and hardships.	Why does Edward's mindset change? What changed inside of Edward during his life?
Narrative of the Life of Frederick Douglass	Fredrick Douglass	4–12	1995	Frederick Douglass	Growth	"Thus after a long, tedious effort for years, I finally succeeded in learning how to write" (p. 58).	Why was Frederick determined to learn to read? How did reading help him in his lifetime?
Out of My Mind	Sharon Draper	5–12	2010	Melody	Melody = Growth; Teachers/Peers = Fixed	Many instances where Melody demonstrates tenacity throughout the book.	What obstacles does Melody face and overcome?
Portraits of Hispanic American Heroes	Juan Felipe Herrera	3–10	2014	All	Growth	All of these "heroes" demonstrate a growth mindset through struggle and resiliency.	The text states that Farragut "would inherit the courage of his mother" (p. 13). Is it possible to "inherit" courage? The text states that Adelina Otero Warren was the "brains of the family" (p. 17). Discuss with students the mindset implications of that statement. Dolores Huerta was told "You don't have the brains for this" by a teacher (p. 49). Discuss the teacher's mindset and the potential impact of that statement.
Shackleton's Stowaway	Victoria McKernan	7–12	2006	Shackleton	Growth	Shackleton demonstrated optimism through every hardship that he was faced. He demonstrated tenacity in all of his attempts to return to the island to rescue the men.	How would the story have been different if Shackleton was a pessimist rather than an optimist?

Ready-to-Use Resources for Mindsets in the Classroom © Prufrock Press Inc.

Book or Story	Author	Grade Level	Year Published	Character(s)	Fixed, Growth, or Both?	Evidence From Text	Mindset Question
Shiloh	Phyllis Reynolds Naylor	4–7	1991	Marty	Growth	Marty will not give up the dog (perseverance).	How does Marty demonstrate grit?
Shooting Kabul	N. H. Senzai	4–7	2011	Fadi	Both	Fadi and his family demonstrate perseverance as they try to find Mariam and as they try to make their new home in America.	Describe Fadi's mindset from the time he fled Afghanistan through the bullying he encountered after 9-11.
The True Confessions of Charlotte Doyle	Avi	5–8	2012	Charlotte	Fixed to growth	At first, Charlotte could not imagine herself doing any physical labor. Her determination and perseverance is demonstrated beginning in Chapter 13.	Charlotte's mindset changed very quickly—from prim and proper to determination and physical labor. What are some of the reasons that this occurred? What is Charlotte's mindset when she returns to the ship at the end of the story?
Unstoppable	Tim Green	4–7	2013	Harrison	Both	Harrison demonstrates resiliency after living in a horrible foster home. Once he is placed in a loving home, he must demonstrate perseverance as he learns to play football and be on a team. He later had to apply those same skills to fighting cancer.	What are some of the things that Harrison learned about himself when he began playing football for the first time? When Harrison lost his leg to cancer, what was his mindset? Cite evidence from the text. What are some of the things he learned from other people that eventually helped him persevere after he lost his leg?
The Voyage of the Frog	Gary Paulsen	7–10	2009	David	Fixed to growth	David shows survivor skills, and doesn't give up.	How does David grow as a result of his experience?
Where the Red Fern Grows	Wilson Rawls	4–7	1961	Billy	Growth	Billy perseveres in raising money over 2 years.	What is the result of Billy's determination and continued effort?
Wonder	R. J. Palacio	4–7	2012	Summer	Growth	Summer's relationship with Auggie shows that she is open to differences and sees the best in everyone.	Would you describe Summer as having a fixed or growth mindset? Find evidence from the text to support your response.

Book or Story	Author	Grade Level	Year Published	Character(s)	Fixed, Growth, or Both?	Evidence From Text	Mindset Question
The Young Man and the Sea	Rodman Philbrick	3–7	2004	Skiffy and his mom	Growth	Even though Skiffy's mom has passed away, he hears her voice in her head saying, "Never give up" and he doesn't.	What can we learn about Skiffy when he says "A thing that's broken can always be fixed, if you work at it. And that's what I intend to do, no matter what" (p. 28)? Why did Skiffy's mom used to say, "The main advantage of being human is the brain, so use it or lose it" (p. 120)?

Ready-to-Use Resources for Mindsets in the Classroom © Prufrock Press Inc.

Growth Mindset Poster

A Teacher's Mindset

There has probably never been a time in education where a growth mindset is needed more. With rapid changes in technology, blended and personalized learning, STEAM, transitions to Common Core, PARCC, and Smarter Balance, it is sometimes a challenge to maintain a growth mindset. Which is why we need to embrace it, be purposeful, and exemplify it in front of our students. We can't be in a position where we teach about a growth mindset and not model it ourselves. We have to be patient with ourselves if we have a setback and speak to a student in a fixed way or emphasize grades rather than effort and growth. It takes time. There are occasions when I notice my own thinking going in a fixed mindset way (i.e., "I will never make the deadline for this book."). When this happens, I do an exercise in my mind that takes that fixed thought and reframes it in a growth mindset way (i.e., "If I write down my weekly goals toward creating these resources and writing the chapters, and stick to a timeline, I will have the book done in time."). The more I reframe my fixed thoughts, the better I get. Imagine that—practice helps!

CHAPTER 9

WHAT ARE SOME WAYS SCHOOL STAFF CAN MAINTAIN A GROWTH MINDSET SCHOOL CULTURE?

Monitoring and maintaining a growth mindset environment is just as important as developing the culture. Schools and districts that are interested in measuring mindset growth with both students and educators can put some things in place prior to any professional learning sessions about mindsets in order to determine the starting point and to measure growth later. This can be done through a combination of observation, anecdotal records, and surveys.

Students' Mindsets

The use of an electronic survey for both the adults and students has proven successful in my experience. Several schools I worked with over the past few years used an electronic survey for all of their students with the exception of those in kindergarten and first grade. The three statements on the survey (see Resource 51, p. 123) were adapted from some of the questions found on Carol Dweck's Mindset Works (http://www.mindsetworks.com). We expect that most students agree with "Everyone can learn new things." The next statement, "Some kids are born smarter than others" will get mixed results—those who agree are demonstrating fixed mindset thinking. For the final statement, "We can change how smart we are," those students who disagree are demonstrating fixed mindset thinking. Students also had a chance to explain their thinking, which was really eye opening. In fact, it was the "why" part of the questions that provided greater insight into their current mindset. Some of the student responses included:

⚙ Some kids are lazy and just too tired for education.

⊛ Everyone starts on zero.
⊛ Everyone is born with the same smartness.
⊛ If everyone puts their mind to something they can do it.
⊛ Kids are not born smart; they become smart.

Kindergarten and first-grade students used "agree" and "disagree" signs (held close to their tummy so their response stays private) when each statement was read and the teacher, paraeducator, or other adult in the classroom would note which students displayed fixed mindset thinking, focusing carefully on statements two and three.

In every school that captured mindset data, it was found that the younger the student, the higher percentage of having a growth mindset. Fixed mindset thinking increased significantly between second and third grade and continued to increase unless an intervention took place. That "intervention" is learning in a growth mindset environment—understanding and practicing the tenants of a growth mindset such as perseverance, resiliency, visualization of neural networks, growth mindset language, etc. Resource 51: Student Mindset Survey (p. 123) is a sample of a survey that can be used for students.

Educators' Mindsets

Measuring adults' growth as a school or district transitions to a growth mindset place is also an integral part of monitoring and evaluating. I investigated already developed tools that measure adult mindsets, but my gut told me that in order to really get a true picture of educators' mindsets, the approach needed to be different so that educators would not subconsciously gravitate toward a "correct" answer. Therefore, something needed to be developed that was based on classroom scenarios and would attempt to capture how an educator would react to specific situations. Would it be a fixed mindset reaction, a growth mindset reaction, or somewhere in the middle (fixed-ish or growth-ish)?

Right around the time I began developing some of these scenarios, Dr. Claire Hughes, Associate Professor of Education at the College of Coastal Georgia, approached me about her interest in finding out which types of teachers leaned more toward a growth mindset: a regular educator, a special educator, or a gifted educator. Claire had also been developing some scenarios and together we solidified a combination of 12 items for educators to respond to, including 10 scenarios and two statements of beliefs about education. Claire was interested in learning about the different types of teacher mindsets, and I was interested in a tool that might suggest a mindset starting point for teachers prior to professional learning sessions. I was also

Student Mindset Survey

Name: _____ Grade: _____ Date: _____

Directions: Do you agree or disagree with the following statements?

Everyone can learn new things. ❑ Agree ❑ Disagree

Explain why:

_____

_____

_____

_____

Some kids are born smarter than others. ❑ Agree ❑ Disagree

Explain why:

_____

_____

_____

_____

We can change how smart we are. ❑ Agree ❑ Disagree

Explain why:

_____

_____

_____

_____

interested in any differences among teachers in schools with different socioeconomic levels, so we added a question about the demographics of the school.

Resource 52: Educator Survey (pp. 125–128) includes the items that were developed for the survey. We created it electronically so it could be accessed from anywhere and data collection would be more manageable. When this was used for schools in a district, I added a menu with the various school names, as well as grade level at the beginning of the survey (as shown in the sample). This allowed professional development educators to customize some of the workshops based on school and/or grade-level needs.

It is very important to send out the survey before staff even hears that growth mindset will be a school focus in order to obtain true baseline data. The same survey can be given again after the school has worked on transforming practices and language as a way to check for growth among teacher's attitudes and beliefs. Of course, what is observed around the school adds to the data collected through the survey. Are teachers providing equitable access to challenge for all students? Is growth mindset feedback and praise heard around the building? Are teachers reminding students about neurons connecting in their brain? Are psychosocial skills such as perseverance, resiliency, and grit being deliberately cultivated in the classroom?

Growth Mindset School Practices

Many schools and districts across the country (and Canada, Australia, United Kingdom, etc.) have embraced a growth mindset culture. Walk through these schools and you will hear teachers praise students' effort, perseverance, and strategies that they use. You will not see students giving up or shying away from challenge. These schools are dedicated to a growth mindset learning environment. However, what often gets overlooked are school and district practices, policies, procedures, and protocols that are fixed mindset oriented. A growth mindset transformation of a school or district must go deeper than growth mindset praise, inspirational signs around school, developing perseverance and resilience, and teaching students about the brain. A systemic review of present practices, procedures, protocols, and processes must occur. Sometimes these practices have been in place for many years and established when educational needs and best practices were different. These practices are sometimes difficult to change because it is the "way we always have done it" or there is fear of pushback from parents. Resource 53: Are Your School or District Practices, Policies, Procedures, and Protocols Growth Mindset Friendly? (p. 129) provides some guiding discussion questions that can be used when reflecting upon and evaluating some of these practices. If it is determined that practices need to change in order to become growth mindset friendly, then frame the change around your commitment toward a growth mindset learning environment. Ideally, parents

Educator Survey

Please indicate your school:
- a. ABC Primary
- b. DEF Elementary
- c. HIJ Middle School
- d. KLM High School

Your grade level(s):
- a. PreK
- b. K
- c. 1
- d. 2
- e. 3
- f. 4
- g. 5
- h. Administrator
- i. Other (please specify):_____

Please respond to the following scenarios according to what you personally would do if there were not outside influences or constraints (system or school expectations) on you. What do you feel is the BEST answer?

1. You have a child who is reading significantly below the rest of the class. Your English language arts class is about to start a text in which she has expressed significant interest. You plan to do the following:
   - a. Give her a book on her reading level that deals with the same topic.
   - b. Have her read the same book as everyone else—she's in this grade level and she has to read this.
   - c. Have her read the book with a small group and provide frequent feedback.
   - d. Have her read the abridged or graphic novel of the same text.

   Explain why you chose this response.

2. A student who consistently gets As in other content areas fails one of your math tests. After determining the student is not having family or personal problems, what feedback do you give him?
   - a. Math may not be your thing. Just try to pass!
   - b. I'm here to help if you want it.
   - c. You might want to change your strategy on how you're studying. You can do this!
   - d. Nothing—the student will have to face the consequences of his actions.

   Explain why you chose this response.

3. Gifted education should:
   - a. Identify students who are truly gifted and give them enrichment or acceleration opportunities.
   - b. Provide differentiated enrichment and accelerated educational opportunities for all students.
   - c. Identify students' interests and talents and provide development opportunities.
   - d. Not exist—all students are gifted.

   Explain why you chose this response.

4. Special education should:
    a. Identify students with disabilities and provide remediation.
    b. Provide differentiated activities for multiple ways of learning for all students.
    c. Identify students who are struggling and provide supported education.
    d. Not exist—all students are special.

    Explain why you chose this response.

5. You have a student in your class who is normally well-behaved. This week, however, she does not stay on task and rarely finishes her work. You are currently studying current events, and you know that she is interested in science. How would you respond to her?
    a. Tell her that maybe current events isn't her "thing" and that next week, you will move on to a different topic.
    b. Give her work to do in science instead.
    c. Tell her that you appreciated the effort she put forth in the discussion.
    d. Ask her how she can see a connection between science and current events.

    Explain why you chose this response.

6. You have a child who has been struggling significantly in your class. On today's test, he did very well. What do you say to him?
    a. Look how smart you are!
    b. I knew that you could do it!
    c. Looks like your hard work paid off!
    d. Nothing—he should be doing this well all the time.

    Explain why you chose this response.

7. You have an identified gifted child who is struggling with reading at grade level. You plan to put her in the following reading group:
    a. The low reading group, so that you can focus on her reading skills with similar students.
    b. A heterogeneous group, so that collaborative learning can be used.
    c. Self-selected groups, each focusing on a different text of interest.
    d. The high reading group, so that she can read challenging material.
    e. I don't group; all children get the same education based on the standards.

    Explain why you chose this response.

8. You have a child in special education who is reading just above grade level. You plan to put him in the following reading group:
   a. The low reading group, so that you don't pressure him and you can focus on his special needs.
   b. A heterogeneous group, so that collaborative learning can be used.
   c. Self-selected groups, each focusing on a different text of interest.
   d. The high reading group, so that he can read challenging material.
   e. I don't group; all children get the same education based on the standards.

   Explain why you chose this response.

9. You have children with the following pre- and posttest scores:

Child	Pretest	Posttest
Noah	70%	85%
Jason	90%	95%
Ryan	10%	60%

   Which child do you highlight as doing good work?
   a. Noah
   b. Jason
   c. Ryan
   d. None of them
   e. All of them

   Explain why you chose this response.

10. You have a child who is identified as gifted and is struggling in your math class. You plan to do the following:
    a. Teach him the math at his level, or collaborate with another teacher to help him at this level.
    b. Teach him the math that everyone else is working on—he's in this grade level and has to keep up.
    c. Have the rest of the class work on the regular assignment and show him more advanced math and explain how the skill you're working on is important for understanding the advanced math.
    d. Have the rest of the class work on the regular assignment and reteach him the original instruction.

    Explain why you chose this response.

11. You have a student in your class with challenging behaviors. She does not stay on task and rarely finishes her work. The only time that she puts forth effort is when the class is discussing a historical or current event. How would you respond to her?
    a. Tell her that she is very smart when it comes to history and current events.
    b. Give her additional work to do in her area of interest.
    c. Tell her that you appreciated the effort she put forth in the discussion.
    d. Ask her why she is interested in history.

    Explain why you chose this response.

12. You have children with the following pre- and posttest scores:

Child	Pretest	Posttest
Noah	70%	85%
Jason	90%	95%
Ryan	10%	60%

    Which child do you feel was the most successful?
    a. Noah
    b. Jason
    c. Ryan
    d. None of them
    e. All of them

    Explain why you chose this response.

Answer Key for #1–#12: A = Fixed, C = Growth

Are Your School or District Practices, Policies, Procedures, and Protocols Growth Mindset Friendly?

School or district leadership teams can use these questions when examining practices, policies, procedures, and protocols through the lens of a growth mindset. A growth mindset practice will have "yes" responses. If the practice leans toward a fixed mindset thinking, should the practice be eliminated or changed toward growth mindset thinking? Some questions to ask include:

➤ Does the practice allow for equitable access—ongoing opportunities for students to access challenging instruction?

➤ Does the practice value motivation, effort, interest, or student work ethic?

➤ Is the practice responsive to the needs of students? (Or does it exist due to tradition or district/school history?)

➤ Does it focus on process and/or growth rather than a cut-off score or grade?

➤ Is the practice oriented to the positive?

➤ Does it eliminate barriers and focus solely on the needs of individual students?

➤ Does it address students' unmet academic needs?

➤ What is the goal of the practice, policy, procedure, or protocol?

➤ Should the practice be eliminated or can it be modified to support a growth mindset environment?

would already be educated in the importance of growth mindset (see Chapter 6 for ideas) and perhaps even on a school Mindset Committee, in which case, getting parents on board will require little effort.

Some of the practices that a school or district may want to review include: policies for participation in advanced learning opportunities (honors courses, AP, IB), honor roll and events surrounding honor roll, grading policies, report cards, policies for allowing students to redo work and retake assessments, student placement, attendance policies, discipline policies, and student grouping practices.

Administrators Planning for Growth Mindset

After participating in growth mindset professional learning sessions, both central office and school-based administrators should be given time to reflect and plan. Administrators can reflect upon what growth mindset practices are already happening in their department or school, plan for developing various components of growth mindset, identify resources that they may need, determine a timeline, and plan for monitoring progress.

Examples of central office goals might include the following. Curriculum and Instruction offices could review materials and lessons that already exist and highlight places within the curriculum where growth (or fixed) mindset discussions and tasks could be amplified. Content area offices could look at places in the existing curriculum where new materials or content can be imbedded; for example, emphasis could be placed on historical figures who demonstrated a fixed or growth mindset or literature in which characters demonstrate fixed or growth mindset thinking could be imbedded (see Chapter 8 for suggested literature).

The office for English Language Learners (ELL) should plan and provide professional learning opportunities for all of their ELL teachers and develop growth mindset lessons that emphasizes growth mindset vocabulary and concepts related specifically to learning English—brain lessons would be great for these kids. Resource 54: Administrators Reflection and Planning for a Growth Mindset Culture (pp. 131–132) is a document that will allow for school administrators to reflect and plan. It also contains a few examples of what each component might look like.

Administrators Reflection and Planning for a Growth Mindset Culture

School/Office: _____ Date: _____ Administrator: _____

Components of a Growth Mindset Environment	A Few Examples of What This Might Look Like	Already Occurring in My Building/Program	Plans for Developing This Component	Timeline	Plan for Monitoring Progress
Growth mindset feedback and praise	➤ ALL staff praise effort, process, strategies, perseverance, etc. ➤ Use of the phrase "not yet" across grade levels ➤ Grading papers—done in growth mindset way—never want to hear phrases such as "you got 8 wrong"				
Deliberately cultivate noncognitive factors that contribute significantly toward achievement	➤ Perseverance is a thread throughout the school ➤ Resilience and grit modeled and recognized in adults and students ➤ Students are "caught" persevering, being resilient, handling difficult situations in a positive manner ➤ Failure is celebrated, looked at as data, viewed as step toward understanding ➤ Students are taught to persist when facing setbacks ➤ Curriculum highlights literary characters, scientists, historical figures that demonstrate perseverance, resiliency, etc.				

Components of a Growth Mindset Environment	A Few Examples of What This Might Look Like	Already Occurring in My Building/Program	Plans for Developing This Component	Timeline	Plan for Monitoring Progress
Equitable access to advanced learning opportunities (responsive instruction)	➤ Preassessment is routinely used across content areas ➤ Teacher-facilitated flexible small groups are evident ➤ Support and scaffolding occurs at all academic levels ➤ Test scores are not viewed as predictors of a student's possibilities and potential; scores demonstrate where some students are at that moment, not where they can go ➤ Frequent formative feedback occurs				
Building an understanding of neural networking in all grade levels	➤ Specific lessons are taught to the students about neural connections ➤ Secondary level—decide when and what subject this will be taught: Health? Psychology? Science? Literature? Freshman seminar? ➤ All teachers refer to neurons connecting to encourage visualization and increase motivation				
Additional ideas:					

Ready-to-Use Resources for Mindsets in the Classroom © Prufrock Press Inc.

"Look Fors" in the Classroom

In *Mindsets in the Classroom*, "Look Fors in a Differentiated, Responsive Classroom" (p. 143) is provided as a way to observe and monitor a school or classroom's journey toward both growth mindset and responsive instruction. What I have learned since developing that sample "Look For" list is that we need to first focus on just those attributes that make a growth mindset classroom. We can't always get to the differentiated, responsive instruction until we have built the climate of growth, effort, resiliency, and possibilities in the classroom.

The development of a mindset-only observation tool for students and adults proved to be more challenging—in part because of what I learned by going into various schools and classrooms to try it out. I identified certain behaviors and statements that I would expect to see and hear from students in a growth mindset classroom and specifically looked for these things. What I learned after visits to many classrooms is that it is not necessarily about what you see and hear, but it is equally important to note what you don't see and hear. For example, in many of these growth mindset classrooms, I never heard one student say things like: "This is too hard," "I can't do this," or "I will never understand this." In fact, in one fourth-grade classroom, the teacher asked the students to draw a picture depicting an aspect of the story they had just read. I listened very attentively as students worked on this task and I admit that I expected at least one student to say something like, "I can't draw!" "This looks terrible," or "Can I draw stick people because I am no good at drawing people?" I did not hear one student say anything about the task or his or her perceived ability to draw—they were all engaged and appeared to be thinking very carefully about what they were drawing. In fact, throughout my visit to many classrooms in this school, I never once heard students say anything about giving up or not being able to do something.

Resource 55: "Look Fors" in a Growth Mindset Learning Environment (pp. 134–135) provides a list of things that could be observed over time in a growth mindset classroom. This can be used by administrators or professional development educators as they walk through their buildings. It can also be used as a reflection tool for teachers motivated to have a growth mindset classroom environment. This is not an all-inclusive list, but provides a starting point for school and individual teacher goal setting. Remember, it takes a growth mindset teacher to have a growth mindset classroom.

Growth Mindset Sentence Samples for Educators

While visiting with a middle school that was working toward a growth mindset environment, I asked the school's leadership team what kinds of resources would be

"Look Fors" in a Growth Mindset Learning Environment

Expectations

➢ Teacher believes that all students can achieve at high levels.

➢ Equitable access to advanced learning experiences exists for all students.

➢ Students and teachers believe in the ability to develop intelligence: students have a conceptual understanding of neural connections.

Cultivation of Psychosocial Skills/Noncognitive Factors

➢ Deliberate instruction/cultivation of perseverance, resiliency, grit, and persistence is ongoing.

➢ Students are given opportunities to safely struggle (not graded) in order to build neural networks and develop resiliency.

➢ Instructional strategies that nurture/promote higher level thinking are imbedded in everyday instruction.

Classroom Environment

➢ A growth mindset class culture is evident—students are not saying "I can't."

➢ Teacher feedback/praise is based on effort, process, and strategies used.

➢ Failure is looked at in a positive light. What can be learned from the error or lack of success?

➢ Grades and scores are not emphasized.

➢ Students are not "labeled" in the classroom: "gifted," "resource," "ELL," "on-level," etc.

➢ Students are given opportunities to set their own goals and reflect on the outcome.

Students Might Be Saying

➢ I don't understand this yet.

➢ My neurons are not connecting yet.

➢ If I practice I will get it.

➢ I am not going to give up.

➢ I can feel my neurons connecting.

➢ Can I try something more challenging?

Ready-to-Use Resources for Mindsets in the Classroom © Prufrock Press Inc.

Teachers Are Saying

➤ You are not quite there yet, but keep trying/practicing.

➤ I like the way you persevere/persist through that task.

➤ Let's think of a new strategy when you try this again.

➤ I am proud of the way that you struggled through that task.

➤ "Yet"

➤ I can see the effort you have put into this and your determination to do this well.

➤ Can you think of a way to make this more challenging for yourself?

Things Seen in the Classroom

➤ Visual reminder/triggers to have a growth mindset (e.g., poster, neurons, etc.).

➤ Students grouped flexibly and working at multiple levels.

➤ Quotes about perseverance and positive reminders about failure.

➤ Displayed student work shows corrections, redos, and growth.

➤ Stickers and displays are effort based.

most helpful to them. Their response was that they would like to have a list of sentence stems or samples that all adults in the building could use as they adjust to using growth mindset language. This list would be available to all adults: office staff, cafeteria, maintenance, etc. Resource 56: Educators' Growth Mindset Sentence Samples (p. 137) is a list of growth mindset sentence starters. This is not comprehensive, but will give school staff a good idea of what we should be saying to our students.

Student Goal Setting

Students of all ages should engage in setting and working toward learning goals too. What a better place to start then setting growth mindset goals? Once students begin learning some of the tenets of a growth mindset, they can begin setting individual growth mindset goals. Some examples of these goals include:

- ⚙ I will work longer at trying to figure something out. I will not give up quickly.
- ⚙ I will have high expectations of myself.
- ⚙ I will ask questions when I can't figure something out.
- ⚙ I will review all of my work and modify or redo it to improve it.
- ⚙ I will no longer think or say "I can't do this" or "I don't get this." I will continue to try or seek help.
- ⚙ I will request time after class to work with my teacher or a study buddy to make sure that I understand.
- ⚙ I will spend time every day practicing _____ skills.
- ⚙ I will try to approach things in a new way if I am not yet having success.
- ⚙ I will ask for more challenging work if the work presented does not require much effort.

Resource 57: My Growth Mindset Goal (p. 138) provides an example of a tool for student mindset goal setting. It allows students to identify one goal at a time and estimate the amount of time they need to work toward the goal. Students must also identify any strategies that they are using to meet the goal and give some examples of how they met or did not meet the goal. For example, if the student goal was "I will review all of my work and modify or redo it to improve it" then an example might be "I completed my chapter questions during lit class and stood up to turn it in when I remembered my goal. I sat down and read each question again and made sure my answers were complete. By doing this, I realized that I had an incomplete answer—this gave me an opportunity to improve my work before turning it in." Resources 58 and 59 (pp. 139 and 140) are samples of completed goal forms. Joseph's example is one where he met his goal, and Catherine's example shows that she has not yet met her goal.

Educators' Growth Mindset Sentence Samples

➢ You are not quite there yet, but keep trying/practicing.

➢ I like the way you persevered through that task.

➢ If you are not happy with your outcome, try again and think about doing it a different way next time.

➢ I am proud of the way that you struggled through that task.

➢ I can see:

   O The effort you have put into this.

   O How determined you are to do this well.

➢ Can you think of a way to make this more challenging for yourself?

➢ I am curious about your mistakes; let's work together to see what happened.

➢ I noticed you used this strategy; tell me a little bit about why you chose to do it this way.

➢ You must be proud of the way you embraced that challenging task.

➢ I see you used a new strategy after the first one wasn't working for you; that was a thoughtful decision.

➢ I am sorry, it looks like I wasted your time on that task; it didn't require much effort.

My Growth Mindset Goal

Name: _____ Date: _____

Growth Mindset Goal: _____

_____

_____

I hope to reach my goal by: _____

Strategies or things I might do to help reach my goal:

_____

_____

_____

_____

Check-In: How am I doing toward this Growth Mindset Goal? Date: _____

❑ I have met this goal   ❑ I have partially met this goal   ❑ I have not met this goal yet

An example of something I did that made me realize that I have met, have partially met, or have not yet met this goal:

_____

_____

_____

_____

Some new strategies to try or my new growth mindset goal:

_____

_____

_____

_____

(If you have a new goal, get a blank Growth Mindset Goal form.)

My Growth Mindset Goal

Name: Joseph   Date: September 7

Growth Mindset Goal: I will work longer when I am trying to figure something out. I will not give up quickly.

I hope to reach my goal by: September 18

Strategies or things I might do to help reach my goal:

Every time I get stuck on classwork or homework I will not automatically quit. I will try to figure it out in a different way or I will use resources like my book to try to figure it out. I will work a longer time until I figure it out but if I can't find the help I need, then I will ask the teacher or my mom for help.

Check-In: How am I doing toward this Growth Mindset Goal? Date: September 14

☒ I have met this goal   ☐ I have partially met this goal   ☐ I have not met this goal yet

An example of something I did that made me realize that I have met, have partially met, or have not yet met this goal:

When I was working on my math assignment in school, I got stuck. Mrs. Davis was working with another group. So I decided to look at the notes on the board again and look at the example on my paper. I tried again and again until I finally figured it out.

Some new strategies to try or my new growth mindset goal:

My new goal: I will review all of my work and add things or redo it to improve it.

(If you have a new goal, get a blank Growth Mindset Goal form.)

My Growth Mindset Goal

Name: Catherine   **Date:** September 7

Growth Mindset Goal: I will not think or say, "I can't do this."

I hope to reach my goal by: September 18

Strategies or things I might do to help reach my goal:

When work is hard for me I will visualize neurons trying to connect in my brain. When I start to think that I can't do it, I will try to persevere until it starts making sense. I will ask for help if these don't work.

Check-In: How am I doing toward this Growth Mindset Goal? Date: September 14

❑ I have met this goal   ❑ I have partially met this goal   ☑ I have not met this goal yet

An example of something I did that made me realize that I have met, have partially met, or have not yet met this goal:

My mind automatically goes to "I can't do this" whenever I feel challenged. I don't want to make mistakes so I give up.

Some new strategies to try or my new growth mindset goal:

Every time that happens I will talk myself out of a fixed mindset and talk my way into a growth mindset. I will remind myself that making mistakes is part of learning something new. I will put a small picture of a neuron on the corner of my desk to remind myself that my brain is getting stronger when I think hard. I will adjust my target date to September 30.

(If you have a new goal, get a blank Growth Mindset Goal form.)

On a visit to a middle school, I noticed that every student had a paw print paper cutout on his or her locker with an individual goal written on it. (The paw print was connected to the school's mascot.) The locker placement was to remind the students of their goals every time they went to their lockers. Some of the goals that I noted included:

- I will practice reading every night in order to improve my independent reading the second quarter.
- I will work to become more organized this quarter.
- I will ask for extra help when I don't understand something in math.

I also noticed that many of the goals were grade oriented, such as, "I will get good grades this quarter." The idea of placing a student's personal goal on a locker is terrific, however, students must be guided to develop a process goal rather than a grade goal. They should think about things they might do: persevere, practice, work longer, seek help, be more optimistic, demonstrate growth, and so forth, rather then focusing on grades, scores, or making the honor roll. The process goals will naturally lead to more success.

Another option is to encourage students to reflect on many growth mindset goals over time. The students can establish the goals themselves or you can provide the goals and they can reflect on them each week, month, or quarter. Resource 60: Student Growth Mindset Self-Reflection (p. 142) provides an example of a tool where students can work specifically toward each goal and determine if they always, sometimes, or have not yet met the goal.

Ideally, monitoring and evaluating a growth mindset environment should be written into your school improvement plans. Year one goals might focus solely on:

- Growth mindset feedback and language
- Teaching students about growth mindset
- Building a conceptual understanding of the brain with students
- Deliberate cultivation of noncognitive skills—perseverance, resiliency, and grit

Year two goals might be:

- Parent education
- Responsive instruction and equitable access to advanced learning opportunities

Using some of the data tool samples in this chapter can provide ways for measuring your school growth mindset goals and contribute to maintaining a growth mindset environment.

Student Growth Mindset Self-Reflection

Student: _____

Beginning Date: _____   Reflection Date: _____

Growth Mindset Behavior	Always/ Sometimes/ Not Yet	Reflection Dates	Examples/Evidence
I reflect on my learning.			
I help set my own learning goals and I monitor my progress.			
I try different strategies if I am not having success.			
I am improving my perseverance.			
I visualize my neurons connecting.			
I reflect on and learn from my mistakes.			
I do not avoid challenging tasks—I welcome them.			
I am becoming more resilient.			
After I have tried different strategies, I ask an adult for help.			

Ready-to-Use Resources for Mindsets in the Classroom © Prufrock Press Inc.

CHAPTER 10

HOW CAN WE USE *MINDSETS IN THE CLASSROOM* IN A BOOK STUDY OR DISCUSSION GROUP?

Mindsets in the Classroom was developed with the goal of being a research-based, educator-friendly resource that would ultimately help children believe in their own potential and possibilities. Many schools and districts have used the book as a basis for book clubs and book studies. The size of the groups partaking in book studies varies: schoolwide, districtwide, schools partnering with other schools, and grade-level team studies. This chapter will offer ideas on ways to guide a book study in order to have active participants who are reflective and open to the ideas that are presented. The following models come from actual book studies that have taken place along with input from the facilitators. Think about the format that makes sense to your audience; school-based groups might choose face-to-face groups in order to facilitate engaging discussions or create a hybrid of face-to-face and online blogging. Partnered schools or districts might have an initial face-to-face meeting to kick-off the study, then transition to an online book study. The following models include examples of elementary, middle, and high school book studies, in a variety of formats, from Iowa, Maryland, and Texas.

Book Study Model 1: Online Blog

Eric Ewald, principal of Riverside Elementary School in Highland Community School District, Iowa, selected a model for a schoolwide faculty book study that requires very little prep time from the book-study facilitator. Using Google Blogger, teachers simply share a quote from each chapter that had an impact on them. After the quote is posted, participants then share why they chose the quote as well as a reflection that may include: further questions they have, instructional implications, how it pertains to their own journey as an educator, etc. At Riverside, the book study was voluntary, 65% of the teachers chose to participate.

One example of how this format played out is a post submitted to the blog by Suellen Swain, a kindergarten teacher at Riverside. Suellen chose the following quote from Chapter 1 in *Mindsets in the Classroom* and posted it as well as her reflection as to why she chose the quote.

> We need to step back, take a breath, and realize that it is not about how fast students master learning. It is about the persistence and effort that they put forth. (Ricci, 2013, p. 9)

> As I read about mindset, it becomes more and more clear to me that although mastering academic content is obviously important, it pales in comparison to mastering perseverance, curiosity, and becoming a learner. If a student learns to approach challenges with perseverance, I believe that the academic content will come. The challenge, of course, is to hold all students to a high level of academic standards, while creating an environment where the pace of learning can be differentiated to allow students to maintain a positive mindset. As I read this book, I feel newly committed to creating this environment. I want to remind myself to "step back and take a breath" and strive to teach persistence and effort.

Teachers at Riverside react to one another's posts and participate in discussions through the blog. Ewald also participates in the same way. As to why he chose this format as a book study, Ewald shared,

> We knew that we wanted to do a book study. I'd had experience with conducting book studies via blog previously. I'm a big fan of the format because it doesn't produce the obstacles that come with trying to coordinate schedules for so many individuals. Plus, there is a lot of flexibility as to where and when each participant participates.

Meanwhile, as teachers participated in the book study, the school counselor, Mallory DeLacy, visited classrooms presenting growth mindset lessons and talked with the children about the importance of perseverance and growth mindset. Teachers who were present during these visits were able to continue the conversation when the school counselor left. Ewald shared that interest grew "organically" through those who observed the counselor's lessons and as a result, conversations began taking place throughout the building. He also shares that the book study blog has gone better than expected and he is planning the next phase, which will be getting parents involved in developing a growth mindset community.

Book Study Model 2: Hybrid: Face-to-Face and Online Edmodo Platform

At a suburban middle school in Maryland, the Professional Learning Teacher developed a hybrid book study for her middle school staff. This consisted of a combination of face-to-face and online discussion using Edmodo that ran in 3-month sessions (every 3 months a different group of teachers would participate). The book study facilitator provided questions and tasks to keep the participants engaged in the learning. She received approval from the state of Maryland for each participating teacher to receive one Maryland State Department of Education Continuing Professional Development Credit for active participation in the book study. (You may want to check with your state department of education to see if it is possible to apply for continuing education credit through a facilitated book study.)

The book study participants worked collaboratively to create a Mindsets Action Plan that was implemented at the start of the school year following spring and summer book study sessions. A number of participants, along with other interested teachers, continue to support the schoolwide implementation of the plan by serving on a monthly Mindsets Committee. An emphasis on relating that learning back to their school community is apparent throughout the book study. Resource 61: Book Study Model 2: Hybrid: Face-to-Face and Edmodo (pp. 146–151) may need to be modified for use in your school or district because it was custom built with this particular middle school in mind. Schools can also use it as a guide to build their own book study, as it is full of meaningful discussion questions and tasks that can contribute to a schoolwide action plan.

Book Study Model 2:
Hybrid: Face-to-Face and Edmodo

Mindsets in the Classroom Book Study

Time frame: _____

Face-to-Face Session 1

Outcomes

➢ Discuss the content and possible implications of developing a growth mindset in our school community.

Agenda

➢ Chapter 1 Discussion

➢ Class Schedule and Expectations

Chapter 1

As you read Chapter 1, what resonated with you . . .

➢ on a personal level as the ideas related to your own mindset and experiences,

➢ on a personal level as a teacher, or

➢ from the perspective of one of our parents?

On page 9, the author states:

The entire school staff—administrators, teachers, support staff—as well as parents must truly believe that all children can be successful. At the same time, children must also accept this belief system.

Share your ideas about possible next steps toward achieving this goal:

Edmodo Discussion Prompts

How this works

1. Respond to each question in a Note. Begin each response with the chapter number so everyone knows which question you are answering. Feel free to pose a question at the end of your Notes to encourage discussion.

2. Please do not post your chapter question responses as a Reply to someone else's Note. This can cause some confusion.

3. After a number of others have posted their Notes, please Reply to two (or more if you are inclined) other posts by clicking on the Reply link.

4. Please post your Notes prior to the due date so others have sufficient time to reply.

   (If any or all of these instructions are confusing, please let me know and I will clarify in person. Thanks!)

Edmodo Assignment Chapters 2 and 3

Due by: _____

Chapter 2

➢ Considering the author's suggestions about how to build a growth mindset school culture, propose some first steps to cultivate a growth mindset school culture at our school.

Chapter 3

1. Paint a picture of differentiated, responsive instruction. What might the components described in Chapter 3 look like in practice at our school?

2. List a few potential roadblocks when designing this type of instruction and offer a suggestion to address ONE of them.

Edmodo Assignment: Chapters 4 and 5

Please read the chapters, respond to the questions below in separate posts, and reply to two other posts on or before _____.

Chapter 4

On page 57, the author states

> Often, the expectations are low for students who do not show strength in the traditional areas of schooling: reading, writing, and math. When students are viewed through a lens of achievement (or intelligence in some cases), opportunities for critical thinking are fewer for those students who are on the perceived lower end.

Question: To what extent to we limit opportunities for critical thinking in our non-"Gifted and Talented" students? Reflect on the author's Critical Thinking Growth Mindset Project described on pages 57–65. Share implications and applications for our work here.

Chapter 5

On page 67, the author includes a quote from *Meet the Robinsons*, "You've failed! From failure you learn, from success . . . not so much."

To support the content of Chapter 5, please watch the video of Rick Wormeli's ideas about failure, growth mindsets, and redos: https://www.youtube.com/watch?v=TM-3PFflfvI&t=122

Question: Share any "a-ha" moments or questions that came to mind as you watched the video. How did what you read and heard challenge some of your ideas and instructional practices? Suggest a possible first step that might help teachers, parents, and students begin to view failure as "information."

Face-to-Face Session 2

Outcomes

➢ Discuss implications and applications of the content of Chapters 1–5 to brainstorm ideas for a Mindsets Action Plan for our school.

Agenda

➢ Chapters 2–5 debrief

➢ Brainstorm BIG ideas, potential pitfalls, and questions to begin to formulate an outline for a Mindsets Action Plan

Chapter Debrief and Brainstorming Session

➢ Chapter 2: Building a Growth Mindset School Culture

➢ Chapter 3: Differentiated and Responsive Classroom

➢ Chapter 4: Critical Thinking

➢ Chapter 5: Failure

Graffiti Boards

➤ On the poster paper provided, please identify BIG ideas from the first half of the book that must be addressed before moving forward with a schoolwide plan.

➤ Make connections with the responses from others and add your questions and considerations on the topics.

Review the template for the action plan. Start to think about a timeline. What should happen first? How? Who will be involved?

Mindsets Action Plan Template

Vision: _____

Mission: _____

Outcomes: _____

Background: _____

Description of Tasks	Persons Involved	Timeline

Edmodo Assignment for Chapters 6 and 7

Chapter 6

Please respond to the following on separate posts and reply to two responses that your colleagues post on or before _____.

We have spent some time already talking about the role of parents in developing a growth mindset culture at our school. You have shared a number of ways to communicate information to the community that can be carried out in the coming year. In addition to sharing information, what small changes or daily practices (either discussed in the chapter or ones you come up with) can be encouraged so parents and teachers can work together to support a developing growth mindset culture?

Check out the video clip from *The Pursuit of Happyness* for some inspiration (see http://www.wingclips.com/movie-clips/the-pursuit-of-happyness/internship-interview).

Chapter 7

Draw from your own experiences and beliefs, and the content presented in Chapter 7, to respond to the chapter title: "Can gifted education and a growth mindset belief coexist?" Support your stance.

Chapters 8–10

Please respond to the following on separate posts and reply to two responses that your colleagues post on or before _____.

Chapter 8 Assignment: This chapter includes many ideas and potential resources that could assist us as we develop our Mindsets Action Plan. As the author suggests on page 98, "Use this as a menu and pick and choose learning opportunities that will be most beneficial . . ." Suggest a brief menu for implementation that includes appetizers, a main course, and dessert options. How will we create smooth transitions between the courses?

(Consider which ideas you would suggest as the author presented them, which you would tweak and which you would replace with an idea of your own? Feel free to include ideas from previous discussions.)

Chapter 9 Assignment: On page 143, the author writes, "To work toward a growth mindset school culture is a commitment that all stakeholders must make." Make one suggestion, unique to each of the following stakeholders, for reinforcing the mindset message consistently. Your suggestion may address a specific audience if you would like (for example, how a teacher would reinforce the message daily with his or her students or with his or her colleagues or with his or her parents), including:

1. the principal and admin

2. department chairs

3. teachers

4. club sponsors or coaches

5. other?

Optional side note: I feel that the Look Fors on pages 143–144 align with the Danielson domains and elements. Do you agree? Do you think it would be appropriate to use this (or something like it) as a resource for instructional planning and/or feedback for informal/formal observations?

Chapter 10 Assignment: Summary. Write a GIST (Generating Interaction Between Schemata and Text; Frey, Fisher, & Hernandez, 2003) to sum up the main message of this book for either you OR the community. One creates a GIST by writing a summary of

20 words that precisely captures the main ideas of the text in a complete sentence. The process helps with comprehending content.

Additional Resources:

Crossfit Perseverance: https://www.youtube.com/watch?v=pE–PRBtoGQ

Born to Learn: https://www.youtube.com/user/iwasborntolearn

Steve Jobs on failure: https://www.youtube.com/watch?v=zkTf0LmDqKI

Famous failures: https://www.youtube.com/watch?v=zLYECIjmnQs

Final Face-to-Face Session 3

Outcomes

➤ Discuss implications and applications of the content of Chapters 6–10 to draft a Mindsets Action Plan for our school.

Agenda

➤ Chapters 6–10 debrief and takeaways

➤ Identify potential roles and responsibilities of all stakeholders to draft a Mindsets Action Plan

Chapter Debrief and Brainstorming Session

➤ Chapter 6: What Messages Should Parents Hear About Mindset?

➤ Chapter 7: Can Gifted Education and a Growth Mindset Coexist?

➤ Chapter 8: What Are Some Ways to Help Students Adopt a Growth Mindset

➤ Chapter 9: What Are Some Ways School Staff Can Maintain a Growth Mindset School Culture?

Graffiti Boards

➤ On the poster paper provided, please identify BIG ideas from the second half of the book that must be addressed before moving forward with a schoolwide plan.

➤ Prioritize the roles of each stakeholder and explore how to actualize the mindsets philosophy meaningfully and realistically at our school.

Review the template for the action plan. Start to think about a timeline. What should happen first? How? Who will be involved?

Book Study Model 3: Middle School
Face-to-Face Department Book Discussion

The faculty at Dr. Douglas Otto Middle School in Plano, TX, came to the conclusion that they wanted to focus on motivating their students to embrace academic challenges and not be afraid of failure. The Leadership Team was already familiar with Carol Dweck's work about mindset but wanted to take things further. As a way to continue the conversation, they decided on a *Mindsets in the Classroom* book study. To kick off the book study, Principal Antoine Spencer invited Plano Independent School District Secondary Teacher of the Year Ramy Mahmoud to speak to Otto staff. Mahmoud spoke about encouraging academic risk taking and creating a metaphoric "foam pit" for students in order to encourage them to embrace challenging tasks. Throughout this process, the teachers at Otto were so inspired that they revised grading and reporting policies to reflect student risk-taking and learning from failure.

Otto Middle School's campus book study on *Mindsets in the Classroom* was designed to encourage teachers to internalize their understanding of the impact of a fixed and growth mindset. Spencer shared, "My goal was for the idea of mindset to permeate how we interact with students, give feedback to students, and in planning engaging and effective learning opportunities." As a result of the book study, Spencer noted, "Our study of *Mindsets in the Classroom* has impacted how we look at students and has given the teachers a focal point as we strive to meet individual student needs."

The book study at Otto required mandatory participation from all professional staff. Each content area department met monthly during its common planning period. These groups range from 5–15 participants and each 45-minute session focused on how the chapter content related to each core or elective content area. Resource 62: Book Study Model 3: Middle School Face-to-Face With Content Area Departments (pp. 153–154) outlines each book study session that occurred for each of the middle school's departments.

Book Study Model 3: Middle School
Face-to-Face With Content Area Departments

Chapters 1 and 2

➢ Teachers take a mindset assessment to determine if they lean toward a fixed or growth mindset.

➢ Neuroplasticity discussion: Teachers are given anonymous student academic data and are asked to determine what influences caused the child to progress academically.

➢ Parent/teacher communication is role-played/scenarios given.

➢ YouTube video: Dr. Julie Schell describes the importance of mindset and how to encourage a growth mindset in students in the video at https://www.youtube.com/watch?v=kW5zT2Yzxb0.

➢ Discussion of growth mindset feedback: Teachers are given vocabulary to use to encourage growth mindset when working with students who are struggling or succeeding easily without effort.

Chapter 3

➢ Each teacher brings a lesson he or she has differentiated to discuss with the group.

➢ YouTube video: Carol Tomlinson provides an introduction to "Getting Started on Differentiated Instruction" in the video at https://www.youtube.com/watch?v=LGYa6ZacUTM.

➢ Small-group discussion questions:

  ○ What is more important, acceleration or enrichment?

  ○ Why does flexible small grouping occur only in reading and primary grades?

  ○ How does differentiation relate to our district curriculum planner?

  ○ Clear expectations are the single most important aspect in managing multiple groups in the classroom. (a) What are students supposed to do when they are done with their work and (b) what should students do when they need help when you are working with another group of students?

  ○ Why do many teachers differentiate for high-ability students at the end of a unit or lesson rather then at the beginning? (For example, students are told what to work on when they are done.)

Chapter 4

➢ Teachers share examples of critical thinking learning experiences utilized in their classrooms.

Chapters 5 and 6

➢ Thinking about failure discussion: Teachers view the "Failure and Success" Tales of Mere Existence video clip from https://www.youtube.com/watch?v=QhsQLPVpMAc and discuss.

- ➤ Socratic seminar: How Can Students Learn from Failure?: Socratic Seminar discussion questions include:
  - ○ What do you think of when you hear the word "failure"? How do your students and their parents feel about failure?
  - ○ What is the significance of failure in a learning community?
  - ○ How do grading or grading policies impact growth mindset?
  - ○ Everyone has failed at something in life. When you have failed in the past, what was the outcome, and how did it impact your mindset moving forward?

- ➤ In *Mindsets in the Classroom*, on page 76, the author states, "If any adult in a child's life communicates low expectations either verbally or nonverbally, then achievement can suffer." How does this statement apply to your work at our school?

- ➤ Reflection quick-write: Teachers respond to the following question: "We are about halfway through the *Mindsets in the Classroom* book at this time. How has our mindset changed how you interact with your students this year?"

Chapters 7 and 8

- ➤ The gifted label discussion: Teachers share their thoughts from Chapter 7.
- ➤ Developing a growth mindset with our students discussion.
- ➤ Brainstorming session: "What qualities do we want to help develop in our students to encourage a growth mindset?"
- ➤ From this list of qualities, work in a small group to create essential questions to guide discussion with students.

Chapter 9

- ➤ What are some ways that we can monitor and evaluate our growth mindset culture?
- ➤ What can we do that will reinforce growth mindset concepts within our curriculum and instruction?

Chapter 10

- ➤ Thinking about all of the ideas, information, and concepts introduced in *Mindsets in the Classroom*, what is your biggest take-away? What is the most prevalent change that you will make in your classroom?

Schoolwide Initiative

- ➤ Creation of advisory lessons based on growth mindset and developing/discussing the essential questions with students.
- ➤ Teachers work in small groups to create the lessons to be used once a week during daily advisory/homeroom period.

Book Study Model 4: Hybrid High School Online Blog Using a Wikispace

Emmanuel André, Staff Development Teacher at Owings Mills High School in Baltimore County, MD, developed a *Mindsets in the Classroom* book study Wikispace, whose introduction reads:

> The purpose is to take whatever lessons we have gained from reading and discuss how to best implement them at our school. For each chapter or chunk of chapters we read, there will be a few questions. Answer them and converse with your colleagues. We will also be creating a unit for the Freshman Seminar Class next year based on this material.

André was able to gain approval for one Continuing Professional Development (CPD) credit through the state of Maryland for each teacher who actively participated in the study. The book study took place second semester, and the group met face-to-face four times throughout the duration of the book study. Resource 63: Book Study Model 4: High School Online Blog Using a Wikispace (pp. 156–158) contains many of the questions and tasks that were developed for the Owings Mills High School book study participants. (It has been adapted for more general use.) Some of the tasks were completed on the Wikispace and others were done in face-to-face discussions. Use this resource as an inspiration for your own high school book study.

Book Study Model 4: High School
Online Blog Using a Wikispace

Chapter 1 introduces the ideas of the growth mindset, the fixed mindset, and neuroplasticity while discussing their overall importance to school culture.

On page 9, the author states: "The entire school staff—administrators, teachers, support staff—as well as parents must truly believe that all children can be successful. At the same time, children must also accept this belief system."

Task for staff buy-in: Identify and post online your input on any of the following in detail:

➢ Ideas that can help us reach the ideal of full buy-in/implementation at our school.

➢ Roadblocks that currently exist that can impede our path to reaching this ideal.

➢ Current structures that exist within our school that could be reappropriated or used to help us reach this ideal.

Chapter 2 dives deeper into the notion of school culture and how specific stakeholder actions can affect student achievement.

Task: Discuss, in detail, methods of feedback you use in your classroom that fit the model the author puts forth in pages 20–21.

Chapter 3 discusses responsive instruction.

On page 50, the author states,

The assessment must match the learning that has taken place for each group or, in some cases, an individual student. If students will be demonstrating understanding through a product, then make sure choices are offered. Grades should be based on mastery of the content that was tailored to the student.

Task: Assessment: What steps are needed so that teachers at our school will be able to move closer to the goal of a responsive classroom through differentiated assessment?

Chapter 4 discusses critical thinking and its importance to a growth mindset.

On page 57, the author states,

Often, the expectations are low for students who do not show strength in the traditional areas of schooling: reading, writing, and math. When students are viewed through a lens of achievement (or intelligence in some cases), opportunities for critical thinking are fewer for those students who are on the perceived lower end.

Task: Do we naturally limit opportunities for critical thinking for our on- or below-grade-level students? Is there a way we can systematically raise them?

Chapter 5 discusses student failure.

On page 69, the author states "It is imperative that teachers develop a climate in their classroom where failure is celebrated and students learn to reflect and redirect so that they can approach a challenging task in a new way or with more effort."

Task: Watch the video: Rick Wormeli: Redos, Retakes, and Do-Overs, Part One (https://www.youtube.com/watch?v=TM-3PFflfvI). How does Rick Wormeli view student failure? Is there a way to institute a late work policy that helps reach this goal?

Chapter 6 is all about involving parents.

On page 77, the author states that "Parents often struggle with the nature/nurture debate and can attribute a child's success to genetics" and "parents often overlook opportunities for helping children learn to adjust to situations when faced with adversity or lack of success."

Task: Identify the common roadblocks our school has historically faced when contacting or working with parents.

➢ What steps can we take to face with those roadblocks?

➢ What kind of growth mindset messages can we send to parents?

Chapter 7 discusses the concept of "gifted" students and growth mindset.

On page 93, the author states: "If students believe that they will, with effort and persistence, be successful in environments of challenging instruction, they are more likely to succeed."

Task: In what ways do we treat gifted/AP students differently than below- or on-level students? Why exactly do we treat them differently? In what ways can we change our schoolwide approach to standard-level students?

Chapter 8 is about helping students adopt the growth mindset.

Task: Consider the current population of our students. What are some ways we can preassess our student's mindset? How would you use this data in your classrooms?

Chapter 9 discusses ways to maintain a growth mindset.

On page 140, the author states,

The learning environment should also be a fear free zone. Fear is such an intense emotion that it can shut down cognitive processes and force the brain to only focus

on the source of the fear and what to do about. The fear of making an error or experiencing failure is a big obstacle to learning.

Task: Choose one to respond to:

1. Think about a student that you have had whom you believed shut down due to fear of failure. What can be done for students like this to ease their anxiety?

   OR

2. Identify a perceived or real source of fear, stress, or anxiety within our workplace.
   ➤ What is the impact of this stress on your classroom?
   ➤ What can be done, on the school level, to help ease that anxiety?

Chapter 10

Task: In one paragraph describe in detail how growth mindset can be used in our building and what next steps should be in place.

Book Study Model 5: A Good Old-Fashioned Face-to-Face Discussion About a Book

All of the above models have served their schools well. They allowed for a deeper understanding of ways mindsets inform instruction and impact students and the school environment. These models also provided opportunities for discussion and reflection. From a personal perspective, when possible, sitting down and talking about a book is an experience that is energizing for me. Resource 64: Book Study Model 5: Menu of Questions to Guide a Book Study of *Mindsets in the Classroom* (pp. 160–161) provides a menu of possible questions that can be asked for each chapter. Choose the questions that make the most sense to you and your staff—those that might overlap with school goals and initiatives or specific needs of the educators within the school. These questions can be used with a partner who is also interested in a book study or with an entire school staff.

Whether you choose one of the models presented here or develop one of your own, be sure that the book study participants contribute to the discussion about where to go when the book study ends. Once the book is read and scheduled discussions are over, a plan should be in place to keep the dialogue going and to develop an action plan for continuing the conversation as well as planning learning opportunities for staff, students, and parents.

Encourage teachers to refer back to the book often for ideas and learning experiences that can be implemented with students. Suggest following social media that will add to their repertoire of resources, perhaps the *Mindsets in the Classroom* Facebook page or Twitter @MaryCayR. Put aside 5 or 10 minutes at each staff meeting for mindset updates—it is imperative to keep the conversation going.

Book Study Model 5: Menu of Questions to Guide a Book Study of *Mindsets in the Classroom*

Chapter 1

➤ We all have areas in our lives where we tend to have a fixed mindset—an area where we think, "I could never . . ." or "I am a terrible . . ."—would anyone like to share one of your fixed mindset areas?

  ○ If you were willing to put in the time and receive instruction and support in this area, could you improve?

➤ If both educators and students had a growth mindset, how would our school look or what changes might you see in our school?

➤ Let's work together and create a Venn diagram, comparing and contrasting fixed mindset and growth mindset behaviors.

Chapter 2

➤ How would a growth mindset environment positively impact our school?

➤ What do you perceive as potential barriers to a building a growth mindset environment?

  ○ What are some ways to address these potential barriers?

➤ Look at the sample letter on page 26. Does our school have similar guidelines in place that create barriers for students with the motivation to participate in advanced learning opportunities?

  ○ If so, what can be done to create equitable access for all students?

Chapter 3

➤ This chapter shares a model for responsive instruction. What pieces of this model already exist in our classrooms?

➤ How are we using preassessment data to meet student needs?

➤ Is small-group, teacher-facilitated instruction occurring at every grade level in every content area?

  ○ If not, why?

  ○ What supports should be put in place to help make this happen?

➤ Does our school encourage equitable access to advanced learning for *all* students?

  ○ Why or why not?

Chapter 4

➤ Why is critical thinking important to a growth mindset class culture?

➤ What are some things that we can do to help students apply critical thinking strategies to a variety of situations?

Chapter 5

➤ Discuss some examples of how our students have learned an important lesson from failure.

➤ What are some ways that we can teach our students to look at errors and failure as "data" or information that will help us?

Chapter 6

➤ What are some things that we can do to communicate the importance of a growth mindset community to our parents?

➤ How can we get parents more involved in our plans for a growth mindset environment?

➤ What components of growth and fixed mindset do you consider critical in parent understanding of the concept?

Chapter 7

➤ In our school or district, how important is the "gifted" label?

➤ Is being identified as gifted the only ticket to advanced learning opportunities?

➤ How might using the terms *gifted* or *GT* contribute to fixed mindset thinking?

Chapter 8

➤ What ideas or strategies from this chapter are you planning on implementing?

➤ What are some ways our school can plan for teaching the entire student body about mindsets?

➤ What are some ways to emphasize these concepts throughout the school?

Chapter 9

➤ What are some ways that we can monitor and evaluate our growth mindset culture?

➤ What can we infuse into our curriculum and instruction that will reinforce growth mindset concepts?

Chapter 10

➤ Thinking about all of the ideas, information, and concepts introduced in *Mindsets in the Classroom*, what is your biggest take-away? What is the most prevalent change that you will make in your classroom or school?

REFERENCES

Alper, D., Clayman, M., D'Esposito, L., Zee, T., (Producers) & Muccino, G. (Director). (2006). *The pursuit of happyness* [Motion picture]. United States: Sony Pictures.

Berger, R. (2012). Austin's butterfly: Building excellence in student work—Models, critique, and descriptive feedback. *Expeditionary Learning.* Retrieved from https://vimeo.com/38247060

Bloch, H. (2013). Famous failures: Failure is an option. *National Geographic.* Retrieved from http://ngm.nationalgeographic.com/2013/09/famous-failures/bloch-text

Bruner, J. S. (1961). The act of discovery. *Harvard Educational Review, 31,* 21–32.

Chesser, L. (2013). The gift of failure: 50 tips for teaching students how to fail well. InformEd. Retrieved from http://www.opencolleges.edu.au/informed/features/the-gift-of-failure-50-tips-for-teaching-students-how-to-fail/#ixzz3XatkdexN

Dweck, C. S. (2006). *Mindset: The new psychology of success.* New York, NY: Random House.

Dweck, C. S. (2010, January). Mind-sets and equitable education. *Principal Leadership,* 26–29. Retrieved from http://www.nassp.org/portals/0/content/61209.pdf

Fisher, D., & Frey, N. (2015). *Engaging the adolescent learner: Setting the stage for 21st-century learning.* Newark, DE: International Literacy Association.

Frayer, D., Frederick, W. C., & Klausmeier, H. J. (1969). *A schema for testing the level of cognitive mastery.* Madison, WI: Wisconsin Center for Education Research.

Grant, A. (2014, October 4). Throw out the college application system. *The New York Times.* Retrieved from http://www.nytimes.com/2014/10/05/opinion/sunday/throw-out-the-college-application-system.html?_r=0

Jones, C. (1994). *Mistakes that worked: 40 familiar inventions and how they came to be.* New York, NY: Delacorte.

National Center for Fair and Open Testing. (n.d.). *FairTest.* http://fairtest.org

Olszewski-Kubilius, P. (2013, October). *Talent development as an emerging framework for gifted education.* Presentation given to the Baltimore County Public Schools.

Peters, S. J., Matthews, M. S., McBee, M. T., & McCoach, D. B. (2013). *Beyond gifted education: Designing and implementing advanced academic programs.* Waco, TX: Prufrock Press.

Ricci, M. C. (2013). *Mindsets in the classroom: Building a culture of success and student achievement in school.* Waco, TX: Prufrock Press.

APPENDIX

SUGGESTED RESOURCES BY AUDIENCE

The following is a list of resources sorted by anticipated audience: teachers, students, administrators, parents and those who provide professional development. Some audiences overlap, so resources are listed more than once.

Teachers

Resource #	Page	Resource
2	7	Important Components in a Growth Mindset Learning Environment
3	8	Classroom Poster
8	22	Teacher Checklist for Planning Differentiated, Responsive Instruction
9	24–25	Checklist for Developing Previews and Preassessments
10	27	Formative Assessment for Learning About the Brain
11	28	Formative Assessment for Learning About Growth Mindset
12	29	Blank Frayer Model
13	31	Differentiated/Responsive Teaching Template for Two Groups
14	32	Differentiated/Responsive Teaching Template for Three Groups
15	36	Feed-BACK Directions

Resource #	Page	Resource
16	37	Feed-BACK Labels
17	38	Concept Placemat for Concept of Three
18	39	Concept Placemats: A Step-by-Step Guide for Teachers
19	40	Concept Placemat for Concept of Growth
20	41	Concept Placemat for Concept of Resiliency
21	43–45	Guess Box Directions, Guess Box Guidelines, and Guess Box Debrief/Reflect on the Process
22	46	Ideas for Items to Put in a Guess Box
23	49–50	Collections
24	51–52	Ordering a Serial Collection
25	54–55	Game Tracker
26	59	Teacher Talking Points on Mistakes and Failure
27	60	Invented by Mistake
28	61	Quotes About Failure
29	64	Failure Videos
37	89	Blank Preassessment of Students' Brain Knowledge
38	90	Neuron
39	91	Neuron
40	92–93	Students Become Neurons
41	94	My Connections . . .
42	96	How Will Your Brain Learn and Grow Today?
43	97	My Strong and "Not Yet" Neural Connections
44	98–100	The Power of Yet
45	101	Diagram of How Neurons Change From Birth to Age 7
46	103	Fixed to Growth Mindset Thoughts/Statements for Students
47	104	Fixed to Growth Mindset Thoughts/Statements for Students (blank version)
48	106–112	Growth Mindset Picture Books
49	113–117	Growth Mindset Extended Texts
50	118	Growth Mindset Poster
51	123	Student Mindset Survey
55	134–135	"Look Fors" in a Growth Mindset Learning Environment
56	137	Educators' Growth Mindset Sentence Samples

Resource #	Page	Resource
57	138	My Growth Mindset Goal
58–59	139–140	My Growth Mindset Goal (student samples)
60	142	Student Growth Mindset Self-Reflection

Students

Resource #	Page	Resource
3	8	Classroom Poster
7	17	Observation of Fixed and Growth Mindset
10	27	Formative Assessment for Learning About the Brain
11	28	Formative Assessment for Learning About Growth Mindset
12	29	Blank Frayer Model
17	38	Concept Placemat for Concept of Three
19	40	Concept Placemat for Concept of Growth
20	41	Concept Placemat for Concept of Resiliency
25	54–55	Game Tracker
37	89	Blank Preassessment of Students' Brain Knowledge
38	90	Neuron
39	91	Neuron
41	94	My Connections . . .
42	96	How Will Your Brain Learn and Grow Today?
43	97	My Strong and "Not Yet" Neural Connections
50	118	Growth Mindset Poster
57	138	My Growth Mindset Goal
60	142	Student Growth Mindset Self-Reflection

Administrators

Resource #	Page	Resource
1	5	Deliberate Cultivation of Noncognitive Factors
6	15	Perceived and Potential Barriers Toward a Growth Mindset Environment
7	17	Observation of Fixed and Growth Mindset

Resource #	Page	Resource
28	61	Quotes About Failure
35	81–82	Guidance Document for Advanced Learning Opportunities: Determining and Planning for Students' Unmet Advanced Academic Needs
46	103	Fixed to Growth Mindset Thoughts/Statements for Students
50	118	Growth Mindset Poster
51	123	Student Mindset Survey
53	129	Are Your School or District Practices, Policies, Procedures, and Protocols Growth Mindset Friendly?
54	131–132	Administrators Reflection and Planning for a Growth Mindset Culture
55	134–135	"Look Fors" in a Growth Mindset Learning Environment
56	137	Educators' Growth Mindset Sentence Samples
61	146–151	Book Study Model 2: Hybrid: Face-to-Face and Edmodo
62	153–154	Book Study Model 3: Middle School Face-to-Face With Content Area Departments
63	156–158	Book Study Model 4: High School Online Blog Using a Wikispace
64	160–161	Book Study Model 5: Menu of Questions to Guide a Book Study of *Mindsets in the Classroom*

Professional Development Educators

Resource #	Page	Resource
1	5	Deliberate Cultivation of Noncognitive Factors
4	10	My Beliefs About Intelligence
5	12	Ways That Mindsets Influence Student Achievement
6	15	Perceived and Potential Barriers Toward a Growth Mindset Environment
7	17	Observation of Fixed and Growth Mindset
9	24–25	Checklist for Developing Previews and Preassessments
26	59	Teacher Talking Points on Mistakes and Failure
36	83–86	Professional Learning Resource: Bright vs. Gifted

Resource #	Page	Resource
46	103	Fixed to Growth Mindset Thoughts/Statements for Students
50	118	Growth Mindset Poster
51	123	Student Mindset Survey
52	125–128	Educator Survey
55	134–135	"Look Fors" in a Growth Mindset Learning Environment
56	137	Educators' Growth Mindset Sentence Samples
61	146–151	Book Study Model 2: Hybrid: Face-to-Face and Edmodo
62	153–154	Book Study Model 3: Middle School Face-to-Face With Content Area Departments
63	156–158	Book Study Model 4: High School Online Blog Using a Wikispace
64	160–161	Book Study Model 5: Menu of Questions to Guide a Book Study of *Mindsets in the Classroom*

Parents

Resource #	Page	Resource
30	67–70	Ideas for Creating a Growth Mindset Environment at Home
31	71	Sample Parent Webpage Screenshot
32	72	Growth Mindset Links
33	74–75	Parent Newsletter Blurbs
34	77	Sample Growth Mindset Bulletin Board
50	118	Growth Mindset Poster
57	138	My Growth Mindset Goal
60	142	Student Growth Mindset Self-Reflection

ABOUT THE AUTHOR

Mary Cay Ricci is an education consultant, speaker, and author of the best-selling education book, *Mindsets in the Classroom*. She was previously the Coordinator of Gifted and Talented Education for Baltimore County Public Schools and an instructional specialist in the Division of Enriched and Accelerated Instruction for Montgomery County Public Schools, MD. Mary Cay holds a master's degree that includes certification in gifted and talented education and administration and supervision from Johns Hopkins University, where she is currently a faculty associate in the Graduate School of Education. She completed her undergraduate degree in elementary education at Mercyhurst University. Mary Cay has experience as an elementary and middle school teacher. In 2010, she received an award for state leadership in gifted education from the Maryland State Department of Education. Mary Cay also serves on the Council for Exceptional Children-The Association for the Gifted (CEC-TAG) board of directors. Her greatest achievement, however, is her three children, Christopher, Patrick, and Isabella, from whom she has learned the most.